LIFETIME Rental Income STREAMS

AN OPTIMAL PROCESS
FOR ACHIEVING IT

Eric R. Judge

Published by Leaping Falls, LLC
Glastonbury, Connecticut

Leaping Falls, LLC specializes in real estate and business.

Lifetime Rental Income Streams

ISBN: 979-8-9965691-0-6
Library of Congress Control Number: 2026915237

Printed in the United States of America

First Edition

For inquiries, permissions, or bulk orders, please contact:
http://www.ericrjudge.com/
jcap2003@sbcglobal.net

Contents

Acknowledgements

Andrea, you make everything easy. Thank you for your love, for being the beautiful and wonderful you, and for your support in encouraging me to tell my story.

Ian, I am so proud of the man that you are, and you now have so many talents. Thank you for lending your marketing talents in getting this book to readers.

My parents, Mae and J. Curtis Judge, for their love and support in molding me into the person that I am.

Greg, Larry and Tony, my older brothers, you each have taught me things which I still reference in my life's interactions with other humans.

Patrick Lyle and Gary Rose, thank you for sharing your time and talents to edit my manuscript. I am eternally grateful for your insightful comments, needed corrections and continued support of my writing journey.

Introduction

The **thesis** of this book is **how to best optimize** your rental property holdings while accepting a comfortable amount of risk. The optimization includes growing your rental properties, increasing **your net rental income, sustaining it and potentially passing it on your heirs**.

The reader will need to take a long-term perspective and a more strategic approach to make the net rental income last a lifetime. That process will require a different strategy than most landlords implement for their goal of receiving net rental income.

While many real estate investors have touted buying a rental property a year and then dying owing it, there are many details that should be considered in those yearly acquisitions and in maintaining your growing rental portfolio. One such detail is what is the best way to die while owning a rental income portfolio. Most only know one way and accordingly, that has been the only way shared. I will share a less commonly known alternative which has become available more recently and it could be a great end-goal with a better pathway that is much smoother with a lot less effort.

In this book, I want to provide a framework to analyze how you go about creating a rental property portfolio, how to extract optimal net rental income and ultimately, to transfer it to the best structure to continue the income flow and to leave it to your loved ones.

Background

I have embarked upon my 20th year as a landlord. It has been a tremendous journey. My rental property landlord and investor journey has not only traversed a few decades but multiple states. At its height my portfolio consisted of properties in multiple states (Connecticut, Georgia, Kentucky, North Carolina and Texas.)

The property types in my portfolio were equally varied. I started with a single condominium and expanded to own many condominiums. Overtime, my rental portfolio also included single-family houses, multi-family residential buildings and finally commercial property.

At one point, I researched how to create a Real Estate Investment Trust ("REIT") with the intent to greatly expand my portfolio during the aftermath of the Great Recession starting in 2008. I bulked up my holdings between 2009 and 2012. I also became very familiar with the rules governing REITS. However, my more conservative nature of risk taking over-ruled my passion for empire building and I folded my "acquisition cards" (a nod to William Poorvu and *The Real Estate Game* book).

My book *Out of Town Landlord – Lessons Learned during the Great Recession* highlights my adventures accumulating properties at that juncture of my real estate investor journey.

Type of Rental Property

What type of rental property do you desire to invest in? A condominium, two-unit, three-unit or commercial building? This decision should be based upon the amount of investment experience you have and your personal strategy for the level of involvement you desire with the properties.

It goes without stating that if you cannot save for a down payment to purchase a one-unit property, then a larger rental property is definitely out of reach for you at that moment. Accordingly, start where you are.

In terms of the level of personal involvement, are you seeking to become a full-time landlord or part-time. As I was in the middle of my corporate career when I started my landlord journey, I choose to be a part-time landlord. That decision caused me to consider how much time could I devote to being a part-time landlord while maintaining my corporate career. As such, I wanted to limit the amount of maintenance and repairs for which I would need to be personally responsible. Purchasing a condominium unit fit perfectly with that goal because the owner has no personal responsibility for outside maintenance.

By investing in a condominium unit, I did not need to worry about replacing the roof, cutting the grass, shoveling snow or anything concerning the outside of the unit as those are considered common area elements for which all condominium unit owners are financially responsible. The collective condominium unit owners, through their condominium association board, delegate such responsibilities to a property management company. The condominium association board is responsible for, amongst other things, hiring a competent and professional property manager to oversee that those things are planned for and are done on an appropriate schedule. See my upcoming book *Investing in Condominiums* for a complete analysis of the many unique attributes of that building structure for net rental income generation.

Perhaps you don't mind or have time for those additional outside responsibilities and would like to purchase a single-family property. Or you have enough savings accumulated to purchase a four-unit property as your first investment.

Multi-unit rental properties have many benefits if they are available to purchase in the area you are reviewing for a potential rental purchase and you have the financial resources to purchase it outright or enough saved and can get approved by a bank for a larger mortgage amount. Typically, banks require a larger down payment for buyers of rental properties.

Multi-unit rental properties provide great efficiencies when it comes to repairs and maintenance. There are potential savings from driving to one location instead of many locations. For example, whether you self-manage or hire a person, you eliminate the multiple trips to different properties to cut the lawn or remove snow.

In addition, the costs to purchase a two-unit rental versus a single-family home do not equate to two times the purchase price of the single-family home. Hence, that lower per unit purchase price will translate into a higher return on investment, all other things being equal.

In addition, there is also a broader base of rental income from which to cover expenses when there is a vacancy. When one unit is vacant, the other unit still might be able to cover the expenses of both units. When you only have one rental unit and it is vacant, you either will pay the expenses during the vacant months from your rental reserve savings account, or you will have to cover them with your personal savings account.

The more rental units you have the larger your expense base of rental income and the greater potential for multiple vacancies that you may be able to cover. This really came true for me when I had my second fire and that property was uninhabitable for two years. The insurance proceeds covered the first year of expenses. The second year my rental portfolio generated enough net rental income to cover the expenses of the property being rebuilt and other rental property vacancies as they occurred.

Summary

The type of rental property you purchase will depend upon your investment budget, personal preference, property types available for sale, and other factors. Included in the decision criteria set should be your return on investment (see chapter **Return on Current Equity** for appropriate way to calculate it).

Finding Rental Properties

You will not have a problem finding rental properties. However, you want to find a rental property that meets your rental portfolio goals. Accordingly, you need to establish the criteria for your rental property. Once that has been accomplished, you are now ready to use the multitude of internet search options available.

MLS® Sites

A good starting place is always the local real estate agent sites. The Multiple Listing Service ("MLS®") sites are controlled by various associations of licensed brokers and their agents. Only association members are allowed to publish real estate listings sales on MLS®.

The National Association of Realtors' website states "The multiple listing service, or MLS®, is a facility that allows real estate professionals to learn about and share local property listings in support of the interests of clients and customers. Realtors® enjoy an economically efficient system of sharing real property information and facilitating cooperative transactions, while their clients and customers have access to the most accurate and up-to-date property information available. There are hundreds of MLS®s across the country, which use a common set of rules to enable a smooth exchange of information in their local communities."

Zillow®

I have used Zillow® the most over the last 16 years. Zillow® can be a good source of property listings and can provide property features, values, rents, historical tax information, historical purchase prices, a few local real estate agents and the property's assigned local public schools. I would suggest comparing property prices with other sources to arrive at the best estimates.

That said, I like that you can not only see the market value but estimated rent. Zillow®'s data can be a good starting point for obtaining other data sources to hone in on the most reliable market value estimates. In addition, it highlights the most recent sales information for similar properties on its site.

LoopNet®

While this website caters more to commercial property, you will find smaller multi-family properties (two to four units) listed here. LoopNet® is also where you will find industrial property and land plots for sale. The multi-family properties are presented in a very professional and useful manner. The website provides you with the current properties cashflows, expenses and net profits. Sometimes having a LoopNet® account will be needed to access such information. Property income data is necessary and important in your ability to ascertain what is the true profit opportunity for you as a future owner of such property.

Crexi®

Crexi® is LoopNet®'s competito and it provides similar data. However, you may find rental properties here that may not be listed on LoopNet®.

Accordingly, spending time on all the available websites will increase the possibility that you will find most of the existing rental properties for sale in the location in which you are searching.

Ultimate Criteria for Searches

Once the rental properties have met your visual and aesthetic criteria, it is time to calculate the net rental income amount. If there is no immediate net rental income after estimating the monthly gross rent minus total monthly expense (include a 3 – 5% estimate for repairs and a 5% vacancy rate expense) or the return on equity (see Return on Equity chapter for proper calculation) is lower than other investment opportunities, don't buy it unless your goal is to primarily to potentially achieve price appreciation by buying and holding it!

Summary

I believe that you should allow the numbers (net rental income and return on current equity) to be silent voters in your decision-making process. This theme is weaved throughout this book. I share that keeping good records, maintaining an updated spreadsheet and analyzing the current real estate market conditions have allowed me to make good long-term strategic decisions for my rental portfolio.

Location of Rental Properties

Do you have a known location preference? Is it in your resident state? Is it in your resident town?

Is it only a certain section of your town? Is there a town or city that has a plethora of rental properties?

Is there a section of your preferred town where lots of new developments are being proposed?

Do local renters prefer certain towns over other towns in your preferred locale? Will renters pay more to live in your preferred town over another town?

Is one town's property taxes so much higher than others? Are one town's taxes so much lower than other towns, and the potential rents are nearly the same or higher in the town with the lower tax rate? Are people attracted to the education system of your preferred town or city?

Perhaps, you prefer to purchase your rental properties in an entirely different state than where you live as I did in the past. Does that state have a growing demographic? Do other states have a higher overall rent potential or do those states have rents trending higher?

Summary

Those are some of the factors for consideration when deciding where you might want your property to be located. While the suggested criteria for choosing a location will be personal and based upon how you want to operate your rental property business, economic factors need to be part of your decision criteria.

Diversification of Rental Properties

Diversification of your rental properties can be thought of in two methodologies. The first methodology or scheme is that you should spread out your portfolio in different locations. The second methodology is to have other types of investments in terms of stocks, bonds, etc. However, this isn't the focus of this book.

By having your rental property in different locations, they may provide you with higher rental income. Even within the same town, certain sections will command a higher rent based upon desirability. That desirability could be based upon the schools or proximity to downtown, medical facilities, pharmacies or grocery stores.

The potential to increase the property value at a faster pace is another reason for purchasing your rental property in different locations. The rationale for that is the same basis as the one for the higher rental incomes.

Additionally, you may want to provide your rental income portfolio with a diversification methodology which may allow you to have properties in locations where tenants and potential tenants may be experiencing the effects of a recession, while your other tenants located in a different state may not be experiencing such recessionary effects.

In 2009, I intentionally diversified my rental property acquisitions by buying in different states to experience the different economic opportunities of those towns, cities, and states where the rentals were located. I continued to be a multi-state operator and strategist until 2021. Read my book ***Out of Town Landlord – Lessons Learned During the Great Recession***. You will learn of my fun adventures crafting, operating and sustaining my multi-state rental portfolio.

We have all seen that each state experiences different economic and population patterns. Leading up to that time Atlanta was booming with business opportunities and attracting many new transplants from other places.

According to Wikipedia's website, Atlanta's population grew from 394,017 in 1990 to 420,003 in 2010 or 6.59% compared with Connecticut's Greater Hartford county's growth of 4.95% which was on a comeback from an earlier population decline.

During that same period, the population growth in the states in which I owned rental properties were as follows: Connecticut 8.73%, Kentucky 17.75%, Georgia 49.54%, North Carolina 43.85% and Texas 49.03%. The southern states were obviously experiencing major population increases. Another area experiencing robust population growth was the Denver, Colorado area at 29.01% while the entire state of Colorado grew 52.65%. My unsuccessful attempts to own property in Denver are well documented in *Out of Town Landlord*. You can't tell me that I didn't try!

Rental Income Differences

In the early days, the differences between the rents that my northern properties could command versus my southern properties were very stark. However, more recently rents have rapidly increased along with the rapid population growth in the southeastern states. The rapid population growth drove increased the demand for leased space. The dramatically increased demand has allowed the associated rents to rocket higher.

As an example of such rental expansion, in 2021 I was able to rent my 2-bedroom Winston-Salem rental for $800 per month in gross rent while my two 2-bedroom South Windsor CT rentals were rented for $1,195 and $1,250 per month. In 2025 the Winston-Salem condominium rented for $1,275 per month while the two South Windsor condominiums could rent for $1,700 per month. Both states fair market rent values increased but maintained the same disparity.

Purchase Price Differences

In September 2009, I purchased a 1,543 sq ft 3-bedroom home in Lithonia, GA for $63,000. Zillow® has that same home listed for $188,000 in 2025. The price for an equivalent home with the same square feet in South Windsor, CT in 2009 was approximately $185,000 and is valued at approximately $411,352 by Zillow®.

In June 2010, I purchased a 2-bedroom condominium in Winston Salem, NC for $61,957.00. An equivalent condominium in South Windsor, CT, would have a fair market value of $110,000. Zillow® currently lists the Winston-Salem condominium's market value at $164,000 while the market values of my South Windsor, CT condominiums are estimated at $188,485. The price differences remain although the gap is not as great as prior.

Ways to Determine Highest Rent per Dollar of Purchase Price

What is a good calculation to compare potential rents in different regions? You can use **cap rate** and the **gross rent multiplier ratio**. Institutional real estate investors use cap rates to determine the most profitable properties to keep or buy. I will show you how to calculate the return on equity in a future chapter. It is similar for providing the highest profitability metric and more appropriate for small investors.

How does the gross rent multiplier ratio work? First, you need to take the potential gross rent and multiply it by 12 (number of months). Then use that number to divide the potential purchase price by. The lower the ratio is, the more rent you get per dollar of property price. It works similar to the PE or price to earnings ratio for providing evaluation of an individual company's stock's price for stock investors.

If we compare my Winston Salem property versus the South Windsor properties, the South Windsor properties currently have a gross rent per dollar of purchase price- *Winston-Salem $164,000/($1,275x12) = 10.72x versus 9.24X for South Windsor ($188,485/ ($1,700x12).* **The gross rent multiplier ratio can be useful for preliminary analysis when looking at one property versus another, particularly in different geographical areas. Its shortcoming is that it does not take the property's actual rental expenses into account.** Your actual costs along with potential rents will be the ultimate factors in determining which potential property purchase is more profitable and provides the highest return on investment.

Summary

Having rental properties in different locations can potentially provide you with lower purchase prices, better returns on investment, faster price appreciation, and a way not to subject your rental portfolio to the same economic impacts during various cycles. In my book *Out of Town Landlord* I provide a more complete discussion of rental property geographical diversification.

To Be a Passive Real Estate Investor or a Landlord

Let's take a pause to consider and evaluate whether it is wiser for you to be a passive real estate investor or a landlord. First, we must establish the definition of each option.

Being a direct holder of real estate involves activity. That means you are not passively earning income but are participating in earning your net rental income.

In order to have the net rental income become truly passive; you must either: hire a property manager, sell the direct holdings and transfer the net sales proceeds using the IRS (Internal Revenue Service) 1031 (code) exchange into a Delaware Statutory Trust, purchase a real estate mutual fund, purchase a real estate company's stock or purchase a REIT. If you are actively involved, you are a landlord.

A passive real estate investor uses their capital to purchase an equity or ownership interest in a property or portfolio of properties, whereas a landlord uses capital to purchase a property to lease to someone for net rental income with the intent to self-manage it.

The landlord will directly interact with tenants, while getting the lease agreement completed or renewed, and operating the property in accordance with the lease provisions. The landlord will contract with all tradespeople when needed and keep track of rent payments, expenses being paid, net rental income and pay all applicable associated federal and local taxes. The landlord will make decisions on what maintenance or renovations may be needed to keep the rental property in optimal condition.

Landlords are responsible for:

1. Finding suitable rental property to purchase
2. Securing a mortgage from a bank unless they have 100% of the cash to purchase the rental property
3. Obtaining great property insurance
4. Getting the property ready for a potential tenant
5. Analyzing current market rents online
6. Seeking potential tenants by creating a for lease/for rent listing online
7. Showing potential tenants the rental property
8. Vetting potential tenants using third party systems which check their credit and crime histories
9. Selecting ideal tenant(s)
10. Getting a viable and legally conforming lease
11. Entering into lease agreement with new tenant
12. Collecting first month's rent and security deposit
13. Repairing broken items in rental property
14. Conducting routine maintenance in rental property

15. Overseeing annual or semi-annual inspection of property or reaping the results of not doing it – Oh, you will regret not doing it!
16. Paying your property taxes on a timely basis or paying exorbitant interest rates or potentially surrendering it to the local taxing authority (read ***To Play, You Have To Be Playing*** chapter)
17. Asking tenants 60 days prior to lease ending date if they will renew it
18. Discovering new tenants if needed
19. Renewing lease agreement with existing tenants

Passive Real Estate Investors are responsible for:

1. Completing due diligence of the investment company, provider, sponsor or property manager
2. Investing their money
3. Collecting net rental property income or investor dividend payments

Hopefully, the highlights above have clearly made the distinction between being a landlord versus a passive real estate investor! In the scenario of being a **passive real estate investor**, you truly receive **passive income**. When you choose to become a **landlord**, you are choosing to be hands on and accordingly, you will **not receive PASSIVE INCOME**. Your **net rental income** is being ***actively generated***.

Summary

It should now be abundantly clear to you that when a real estate advertisement or commercial tempts you with the lead-in of "How to Make Passive Income", that it is a misnomer **if you will be actively engaged** in the management of a rental property. In that scenario, you are a **landlord** and there is **no** such thing as **"Passive Net Rental Income!"** You are now well informed, have a stronger understanding of passive income and are fully prepared to make the appropriate distinction.

Property Management

Now with the clarification of landlord versus real estate investor out of the way, let's address different ways to manage your rental property.

One of the fundamental values that I incorporated into managing my rental properties from the beginning was to be a "fair and firm" landlord. What on earth does that mean? I can hear the chuckles and, even louder, the skepticism. I hear it – A fair landlord? There is no such thing!

I truly believe, and I have heard from many of my tenants, that they have enjoyed their interactions with me. So much so, they are still connected with me via Facebook or sending text messages directly to me during the holidays.

I have very thoughtfully built my landlord reputation around the principles of being fair and firm. Now, before I start guiding you down the tunnel of landlord "**fairness**", please know that I entered my real estate journey as a businessman and business is the lifeblood of my processes.

It is within the orchestration of my processes that I execute the **"firm"** part of my landlord obligations. Yes, obligations. If you forget to implement them, a tenant, their attorney or a government agency will remind you how to do it (*Out of Town Landlord* has a great story about a tenant wielding the BIG Brother (governmental agency) stick at me fiercely, but under false pretenses).

Good Chips in the Tenant Cookie Jar

Over two decades, I was often astounded when a tenant would tell me that their prior landlords never did some of the most basic things. For example, I always explain at the beginning of any new lease term that I want to know as soon as possible when something breaks. Then, I will get it fixed pronto without asking hundreds of questions, and without trying to assign any blame for what was broken.

Many of the tenants who had experienced landlords who wanted to keep every penny of rent by not making repairs, would be very reluctant to follow my requested process. When they finally called me about a repair, they would tell me about two or three other things that needed repairs long ago. Over time, they would create the new behaviors that I requested, and they would see that I meant what I said to them earlier and things were repaired quickly, professionally and with a thank you from me.

By the time most tenants left my property, I had earned their respect, and many have stayed in touch as I have previously mentioned. That is rewarding in and of itself. However, I have gained additional benefits from living those principles.

The best example is when I had to sell 4 properties. The cooperation of the tenants living in those properties was unbelievably excellent!!! They were so flexible with allowing the property showings for the multitude of people looking at the properties.

They agreed to shorten their leases to accommodate me selling the properties. Additionally, they would ensure that the place was spotless for showings. Equally important, all their actions were completed in the most pleasant manner.

When I was selling my last two residential rental properties, those tenants wanted to be in their home when potential buyers came. They were very patient and civil with the process of selling the properties. Originally, I was nervous about them being present with potential buyers. If the tenants' behavior was not professional, it could harm potential sales.

What happened was the total opposite. In each instance they enhanced potential sales by providing useful information to potential buyers. They would even communicate with me about who they thought were really interested in buying the places. In the end, they told me prior to the real estate agent who would be putting in an offer, and those forecasts were 100% accurate.

I could go on and on about all of the wonderful benefits that I have been given by tenants over the years because of my "Good Chips in the Tenant Cookie Jar".

Oh, you ask **what did the tenant get in return for their accommodation to me?** They received **5-Star Landlord services**. Yes, I pride myself on being a landlord who keeps his rental property in impeccable condition, who fixes things as soon as he is told that they are broken, who tries to fairly accommodate people when bad things in life truly happens to them, and who fairly implements reasonable rent increases.

Property Management Processes

What follows are some of my core property management processes:

Create incentives for tenants to stay with you longer with **multi-year leases** – Once you have done the work to find and secure a good tenant, keep them as long as you can. The way to do that is to present tenants with a multi-year lease that has a rent increase spread over many years which in aggregate are lower or equal to the one-year rent increase. I have found that **long-tenured tenants are the most profitable tenants and the multi-year lease option better incentivizes them to stay longer than** a standard one-year residential tenant lease, a rent increase or no rent increase.

Limit or eliminate turnover time between tenants by showing the rental unit while it is still occupied. You will need a provision in the lease which allows you to show it to prospective tenants by giving the existing tenant at least 24-hour notice prior to the showing time. Then, schedule multiple prospects on the same day with the appointments right after the other so they know there is competition. Such scheduling also allows you to be more efficient with your time. Creating and sending the tenant a Move-Out Expectation Letter (see below) will also reduce turnover time between tenants.

Continuous Maintenance - Whether the tenants call for repairs or not, implement a plan to replace certain items periodically that will wear out over time. Think: garbage disposals (every 5 years), all types of filters, water heaters (5 to 10 years) and smoke detectors (every 10 years).

Upgrades or improvements every 10 years – Regardless of whether they work without fail, no one wants to rent an apartment where all the appliances are 20 years old. Plan to replace appliances and paint the space at least every 10 years. Otherwise, you will have to discount your rents substantially versus market rents. As a good safety rule, change the smoke detector batteries every year if applicable as many new ones have a 10 battery.

Small but continuous rent increases which keep up with inflation and market rents. The balancing point is to manage increases so that ideal tenants don't leave. Some landlords don't raise rents for years. This seems like a good approach until you have priced your rental units several hundred dollars below comparable rental units. Tenants expect increases, they just don't want them to be large increases. Target increases close to inflation or the increased amounts for property tax, insurance or other expenses to try to maintain a certain return on equity.

Evaluate market rents on an annual basis – This must be balanced and part of the consideration of what your rent increase can be. You will not be able to implement $100 per month increases with your tenants if market rents have decreased and you are right at the market rent for your location prior to the proposed increase.

Make sure your best tenants know that you appreciate them and how they take care of the property. You must tell them in person, via letters or with small gifts at holiday time.

Get multiple bids on larger projects and repairs. However, building a relationship with a few tradespeople within each specialty can be helpful in emergencies and other situations. The cheapest price should not be the only thing considered. Many tradespeople will reasonably price things, once they know you will be a loyal customer.

Move-Out Expectations Letter (see Appendix). I copied this idea from Mr. Landlord, Jeffrey Taylor, and it changed the amount of work that I need to do between tenants and drastically reduced my turnover time as the tenant does the majority of the needed cleanup and that is exactly as it should happen. Afterall, they created the need for it.

Remember that each tenant was provided with the rental property clean and in good working condition. It is only fair that they leave the premises as they found it!!! Otherwise, charge them for the labor and materials needed to get the place in presentable condition. This letter is part two of my one-day tenant turnaround process. Part one is introduced under ***Lease Agreement.***

Different Ways to Manage

Out of Town Landlord – Lessons Learned During the Great Recession clearly details the advantages and disadvantages of self-management versus hiring a property manager.

If you have been a landlord or real estate investor for five years or more, you probably know which is your preference by now. I would still suggest that you re-evaluate whether that is the appropriate path for the current juncture you are at as things change. With changed circumstances, there should come a period of new evaluation.

Considerations for Self-Management

What is your **Emotional Quotient** for managing/dealing with people? If it is high, you might be more inclined to self-manage your properties. If it is low, you should honestly assess your ability to increase it before choosing to self-manage.

Available Time – Do you have the available hours to assign to managing rental properties? How will managing your rental properties impact your coupling time or time at children's activities? Would your extra or available hours be more productively used by acquiring skills which could increase your hourly pay for work? Would using those extra hours at your current job bring you more recognition and a promotion with incrementally higher income than any potential net rental income projected in your current spreadsheet projections (see Current Return on Equity chapter)?

Do you have **adequate property management knowledge**? Are you willing to spend the time and/or money to acquire sufficient property management knowledge? Everyone who has ever lived in a home thinks that experience automatically qualifies them as an expert. It does not. In fact, that incorrect perception could set you up for failure or, at a minimum, lots of misery.

Considerations for Hiring a Property Manager

What is the professional manager's tenure as a property manager?
How do they want to be paid?
How many properties do they currently manage?
How many people do they have assisting with the management of those properties?
Do they know lots of tradespeople?
Do they have an internal trades staff?
How are those trades people compensated?

Most property managers offer **comprehensive property management** services. However, I have worked with several real estate agents that **only find and screen tenants.** Comprehensive property management services entail finding the tenants, screening them, approving them, getting the lease agreement executed, collecting rents, finding tradespeople for repairs and maintenance, handling tenant issues and sending the net rent to the property owner.

I used a real estate agent in Atlanta named Rosalind, who would do a wonderful job finding and screening prospective tenants. After that, she would mail a set of keys to me and provide me with the tenant contact information. She also allowed me to leverage her tradesperson network when I needed to complete maintenance or repairs.

In Winston Salem, NC, I had a similar relationship with a real estate agent who said that I was the only one for whom she supplied such limited services. All of her other clients were provided with comprehensive property management services. Additionally, she would supply a punch list of needed repairs and offer that her handyman husband could complete them for a reasonable price. I would usually oblige her offer, and her husband would complete the work well.

One Bad Experience - Let me share a real property management story. In **Texas** my first two **cowboys**, I mean property managers wanted to take me for a little bareback horse "ride". After a few months with them managing my two 4-unit buildings, things start breaking. One month it was a dishwasher not working. The second month the washing machine needed new parts. The next month it was something electrical. I started thinking about how often repairs were needed at my Connecticut rental properties which I owned and managed. I had never seen so many repairs needed in a short period of time for properties that are about ten years old. Then a thought shared by John T. Reed in his books came to me. Mr. Reed shared that there are some property managers who take "kickbacks". The first way kickbacks are generated is when a fabricated invoice is submitted. There actually are no repairs needed in the rental unit. Then the property manager keeps the money billed on the false invoice. The other way that it is done is when there is an actual repair needed. In this scenario, the property manager tells the repair person to increase the invoice by some amount which is then split between them.

On October 10, 2010, I wrote in my notebook that one of those property managers called me to notify me that one of the four tenants in that building was being evicted. I ruminated that the tenant had only been in my property for two months. What poor screening of the tenant was performed by the property manager? In addition, that news was coupled with my other Texas property having a high vacancy rate over the prior two months.

I began to think that I needed a new management strategy for Texas and that I was going to take these rentals from them to manage myself. My thought was to go all in by starting a property management company focused on my Texas properties. After all, "I was confident that I could run a property management company like the best landlord would manage their own rental properties." Needless to state, I fired them.

Summary

The property management process is where all the pieces come together. Done properly you will grow your net rental income and sustain it. Done poorly, your net rental income will not keep up with the market and your ultimate return on equity will be low. You don't want to be a real estate investor who allows their property to diminish into a less than desirable living space. That will ultimately have a negative impact on the purchase price appreciation of your rentals during the time you own it.

Finding Tenants

The internet has not only made finding tenants so much easier than when I first became a landlord but has also increased the number of potential tenants one can find. There is Zillow Rental Manager, Apartments.com, Craigslist, and many more. In the beginning you should use a few of them. During that testing period, you will learn whose services you prefer.

Tenant Screening

There are many tenant screening services. Some of the rent payment portal service platforms which I highlight in the Electronic Payments chapter of *Out of Town Landlord* also perform tenant screenings. I have used Tenant Verification Services and Transunion's SmartMove. I found both to supply the requisite screening criteria and evaluation.

When I started leasing my rental properties to tenants, I would collect a potential tenant's address, cell phone number, driver's license, birthdate, social security and other personal information. While I kept that information in a Sentry Safe and my home had an alarm system, I never got comfortable having such sensitive personal information.

Sometime about ten years ago, the tenant screening services figured out that the tenants also preferred for landlords not to hold such sensitive information. That is when they became the obtainer of the birthdates and social security numbers. Thereby, allowing the landlords to not have to obtain such information. In fact, many of the vendors only ask the landlords to provide the name and email addresses of potential tenants solely.

The screening services vendor then sends a secure portal link to the potential tenant. The potential tenant then opens the email message, clicks on the link and goes to the vendor's website. At the secure website the potential tenant enters their sensitive identification information and other information like former addresses. Then the screening services vendor creates reports which include credit history, criminal background and some have landlord histories, if prior landlords have submitted that information.

Summary

I really like the evolution of the tenant finding and tenant screening vendor service industries. They have made the landlord's task of finding qualified tenants much easier. The number of providers in each segment continues to grow. With the increased number of options, there has been an increase in the services offered.

Tenant Hall of Fame

I have been so fortunate to have so many absolutely wonderful tenants. In the early days I created my "Tenant of Fame" in which I inducted tenants mentally. They remain connected to me via FaceBook and send text messages to me around the holidays.

This chapter will now memorialize them forever as I induct them into this book. I have changed the names as there were too many to track down to gain their permission for inclusion in this book and there are also a few tenants who are being inducted by virtue of them not being so nice with their extremely memorable deeds.

My Rookie Season

My first tenant taught me so many landlord lessons. At first, I thought that I had hit the jackpot as my first rental property came with tenants included with it. I did not have to hunt for them and ***voila***, the rent showed up on time – at least for the first few months.

This tenant happened to be receiving Section 8 Housing Vouchers. Section 8 Housing Choice Voucher (HCV) Program, commonly referred to as Section 8, is sponsored by the Department of Housing and Urban Development. The Section 8 Housing voucher program gives a voucher to recipients to help them afford non-government provided housing. Local town or city housing agencies facilitate the distribution of the Section 8 Housing vouchers to recipients with low income, are disabled or are seniors.

There are landlords who absolutely love tenants with Section 8 Housing Vouchers and those who will not accept tenants who paying rent by using the program. Those who absolutely love it, typically like that rent is guaranteed by the government while the recipients qualify. Those that don't like the program believe this cohort of tenants are more trouble than tenants who are eligible for the vouchers. I have had more great Section 8 tenants than not. Later in this chapter you will read about one of favorite tenants who was in this program.

Now, back to the story of the tenant from My Rookie Season. After a few months, all of the "fun" started as their teenaged son decides to climb through the neighbor's window for the fun of it and, obviously, without permission! Of course, you know what will happen next. The police get involved and there are associated police reports.

Well, the late rent check payments eventually wore me down and I let them know in my own way, it was time to vacate my rental property. Their tenure was two years. The worst part was they left one interesting task for me with their vacancy.

What's that brown stuff that took me five major cleanings of wiping down the entire wall to remove it? I questioned the landlords in my real estate investment club whether they had to do such cleanings for smokers. All said no! Also, please keep in mind that the lease agreement did not allow smoking in the unit.

Then, one landlord strongly suggested that I think of other very addicting substances that were being smoked by people who had gotten into very bad human states of living. With that statement many things done by one of those tenants began to make more sense to me.

2nd Tenant

She was a single professional woman who kept the place neat and clean. She always paid her rent on time. It was a coincidence that she was working at the same company as me. I did not know that fact until one day I saw her in the cafeteria. The reason that I did not know that information prior to then was that I didn't have to run her credit and obtain background information from her as I inherited her in the purchase of the rental property from the prior landlord.

Toilet or Garbage Can

The primary issue with this tenant was that I had to constantly send the plumber to that property as, unbeknownst to me, everything was being sent down the toilet. There could have been a potential culture issue at play.

What I know is that I was left pondering whether they had used toilets before? The plumber found banana peels, toys, etc. This experience resulted in me adding an provision in all my future leases that, except for regular toilet maintenance or the pure nonfunctioning of the plumbing, the "tenants are responsible for clogged drains due to hair buildup, food or any other waste caused by the tenant." There!!! That lease agreement provision solved the issue for me having to deal with such for all future tenants!

This tenant came with other issues which were not any lighter.

The next episode of this bad situation was blood on the bathroom walls and red dye all over the new carpeting.

While the situations mentioned thus far had me miserable, my final discovery of how they had been inhabiting my rental would haunt me for many months after they left my rental unit.

My final revelation about how they had misused my rental was that one of their children couldn't or refused to make it to the bathroom and continuously peed on the carpet near his bed. Once they moved out, I doused the carpet with pet odor cleaner in an attempt to remove the pee odor. My many attempts to eliminate the odor were fruitless as it would come through on damp and rainy days. Consequently, the carpet and floorboards had to be removed to finally get rid of the urine smell.

I couldn't make up these events even with my most unrestricted imagination. Prior to them happening in my rentals, I would not have been able to imagine them. I am just not that creative.

Lovely Recent Immigrant Family

I had the pleasure of securing a lease with a family who recently arrived from India. The father was a professional, and the mom was a homemaker. The two children were going to attend the local high school. The two to three years they rented from me were just delightful. I thoroughly enjoyed all my interactions with them.

They saved enough money to move out of my rental and to purchase a home in the same town. They were the ones who would alert me to my condominium unit burning as they saw it on the news. I remain in contact with them to this day.

Wonderful Teachers

They would send wonderfully handcrafted cards with thoughtful messages every month along with a check. How do you top that one!! Talk about how to earn favors with your landlord.

Now the reader should keep in mind that my monthly process and practice of receiving checks ended for me around 2015. In 2012, most of my tenants began making their rent payments directly into a bank account created solely for that purpose, through Zelle and PayPal as those options became available.

Read the Electronic Payments chapter for the benefits of these payment methods.

My young teachers remained for almost 5 years. They moved out to purchase a home. Later they expanded their family with three children, a boy and twin girls. I get the joy of seeing them grow as a family on FaceBook.

Professional Delinquents

Having a couple with both working nice paying white-collar jobs would seem to put a landlord at ease. However, that was not my experience as my pair of professions did not pay the last two months of rent and were frequently late paying rent.

What was also insulting to my landlord sensibilities was that the cat peed in the corner of my beautiful wood floors and tore the window blinds. It was the only pet that I had allowed in that unit. That consequence which I had to face for breaking my foundational rule of not allowing pets, by making an exception for them, was also a reminder to relentlessly adhere to my foundational landlord rules!

Key West Bob

He was a transplant to Georgia. He earned a salary of approximately $85,000 per year in 2010 dollars and equivalent to $126,288 in 2025. He had no children or other dependents, yet he was always late with the $1,200 monthly rent. His excuses were always that someone died who needed assists with their funeral expenses and his car was damaged in an accident resulting in his car needing repairs. I viewed these excuses as the equivalent of the schoolkid who arrives in his classroom without his homework and tells his teacher that the dog eat it.

What I discovered was that he was renovating my condominium unit as though he owned. Yes, as though he owned it – he did not ask me permission nor get my input to conduct renovations. He painted over my nice cabinets which were less than 10 years old, and he removed all the carpeting upstairs and downstairs to put in the luxury plank floors.

The truth is that I would have gladly shared in the costs of those renovations if he had communicated with me about his desire to do them. However, he wouldn't have gotten my approval to paint the cabinets which didn't need it. Furthermore, I absolutely abhorred the pastel color he painted them. Luckily, the next person renting the unit and who ultimately purchased it, loved them!

Very Nice Young Couple Loses Everything

I was so proud of the wood floor that I refinished in the second bedroom of one of my rentals. It was a dark brownish-red finish which the wife loved. I discovered the hardwood floor under the worn-out fraying carpet and decided to refinish it myself. I painstakingly polished those floors multiple times, put on a few coats of stain and a nice coat of polyurethane. I was so proud of the results of my first floor refinish!

Unfortunately, my first "floor refinish masterpiece" was destroyed in my second fire (read Property Insurance chapter of ***Out of Town Landlord*** for the details).

Even worse was the fact that the young couple lost all their earthly possessions in the fire. The figurative "salt" added to their open and fresh wound was that they did not have renters' insurance which would have only cost them $12 -$15 per month at that time. If they had only sacrificed some other monthly expense to purchase a renters insurance policy, they would have been able to replace everything without any further cost.

While I don't know the facts about what ended their relationship, I do believe the fire losses that occurred on Saturday, November 5, 2016, caused irreparable harm to their union as when I ran into the guy about two years later, they were divorced, and he was coupled with someone different.

Professional Transplant Hustlers

After refurbishing one of my condominiums two and a half years after a fire destroyed it, every inch of it was simply beautifully rebuilt. I rented it to a family with two children that had transferred from the Midwest.

One day I received a call from the wife of the couple. She told me they were being laid off. I asked them to share the notice detailing their layoff process with me. I never received it, nor did I hear anything else about that matter afterwards.

They had only stayed renting from me for a year and tried to get a break on rent during Covid, even though they were both securely employed and working from home like millions of other families in the United States.

Younger Brother Wants to Spread His Wings

I had one of the nicest experiences renting to a young guy who had been living with his sisters and wanted to start being more independent by moving out of his sister's place. All my interactions with him were just so pleasant. He showed me respect as though I was his uncle.

He stayed with me for two and half years. I remember him working lots of hours including two jobs to afford living on his own. I allowed him to be late with rent twice due to his older car needing repairs. However, he told me exactly when he could pay it and he paid it exactly then.

I remember being a little sad when he told me that he wasn't going to renew the lease as he could not afford to continue living by himself. I told him that I understood and wished him luck with his future.

Purple Walls and Guns on Display in Georgia

I could have started my Hall of Fame Tenant list with this tenant as she caused me the greatest emotional stress and loss of money. However, I did not want the worst tenant that I encountered to overshadow all the wonderful ones who I encountered.

Where do I begin? Hmmm?

Everything was going along nicely, until a tradesperson did a shabby job on a few repairs. She shared her concerns with me, and I hired a different person to get the job done correctly.

The last person that I sent to repair the master bathoom shower door reported to me that "my tenant was crazy." I asked him why he said that. His response was that she was trying to tell him how to make the repair and as he was leaving, he noticed that she had placed her guns on the bed for him to see. The handyman said to me "I've got guns too and the next time that I go over there I will have them on me". I remember thinking **"there is going to be an "*O.K. Corral*"** event in that condominium with them shooting each other to death."

Even though everything was fixed correctly, she somehow attributed the original tradesman's shabby work product to me as a landlord and things were always more difficult after that incident.

Then the dishwasher broke and I replaced it with a new one. In addition, she complained that the kitchen cabinet door did not close properly and that they were mismatched. I replaced the cabinet doors so that they were all-conforming.

In November of that year, she sent an email message to me stating that the heat would not go above 72 degrees Fahrenheit. I sent three different heating and cooling system professionals and they all agreed on the genesis of the problem. She was setting all thermostats in the condominium above 72 degrees at the same time. The heating and cooling tradesmen said that the system was installed less than 10 years earlier and was not built to sustain that capacity.

The next thing I know is that I am being contacted by the City of Atlanta Health Department for not providing my tenant and her fictitious minor niece with heat. I supplied the health department official with my invoices and a written statement from the heating and cooling professionals that heating system was functioning perfectly.

It was then that I realized that I was never going to be able to please her, and her attitude was not going to improve. Consequently, I did what any reasonable landlord would do. I made a business decision to send her a letter stating that I would not be renewing her lease in February and that we should agree on a move-out date.

She subsequently refused to pay January's rent. I sent her a Pay or Vacate letter. She said that she paid the rent. I started the eviction process.

Once I received the property back five months later, I learned her parting gift to me was that she painted a few of the rooms dark purple. I could have only wished that her story ended there. However, then she sued me for not returning her security deposit (I kept it. Rightly so, as she owed me a few months' rent and ruined my property). I made three appearances in the Fulton County Courthouse before I hired an attorney. It would be two years before I unentangled myself from the Georgia Court System (read Lawsuits and Time in Court chapter *Out of Town Landlord*). My real estate professional had picked someone who knew how to navigate that court system like a pro.

I spent money on airfare, attorneys, cars, sheriffs and the time lost which could have been put into more productive pursuits.

Impatient Duo

I rented one of my rentals in Fayetteville, NC to a father and his son. After being in the condominium for about one year, they called my property manager and informed her the dryer was making a funny noise. She told them not to use it, and that she would send a repair person to fix it soon.

The next day they ignored her request for them not to use it and then put a load of clothes into the dry. The dryer started sparking electricity and the sparks ignited the clothes. The flames on the clothes got larger and seeped out of the dryer into the condominium unit. The condominium unit became engulfed in flames, and they ran outside and called the fire department.

The fire department came and doused the condominium unit with water. The fire had spread to the unit next door, and they were spraying it with water. They put the fire out but amid doing so, they totally soaked the two units below with water. Consequently, four condominium units, including mine, were totally uninhabitable.

If the father and son had patiently waited until the dryer was fixed or replaced, I would have never experienced my third fire (read the Property Insurance Chapter of *Out of Town Landlord* for the entire story) and lost the use of my rental for a year and a half.

Young Doctor in Winston Salem, NC

This one is short as the young doctor did everything perfectly. He performed my Landlord Rule One Perfectly. It is not what you think. It is that you must communicate whatever is happening in the rental. He called or sent an email message whenever something was broken. He paid his rent on time. When it was time for him to finish his residency and move to a new city, he communicated with me far in advance of the lease notification period. He was fantastically easy!!!

I Don't Need a Lease Agreement with You

A woman who was the cousin of my authorized tenant decided to move into my condominium unit without my knowledge. When I realized that someone other than my authorized tenant was living there, I attempted to contact her. She initially was nice and compliant.

I explained to her that my lease agreement did not allow for subletting and clearly states that each potential occupant is required to be approved by me. The approval process included completing an application, submitting to a credit check and entering into a lease agreement directly with me.

She originally agreed to complete the items in my required process. When I did not receive any of the items after a week, I called her. Now she stated in very clear and very certain terms that she did not need to sign a lease or do anything else that I requested as she had an agreement with my tenant. I was aghast at her bold and adamant refusal to cooperate (see Vacate Letter mailed to her in Appendix).

Well, I regrouped and thought this is a **mission for Alpha Evictions**. By now this vital service was more than worth of every dollar which I paid them (read how I was introduced to their services in the Lawsuits and Time in Court chapter). They had her removed in a few weeks and I rented that place to someone else very promptly.

Wonderful Couple with Tweener Princess Stays for 5 years

Sometimes you just get lucky. The couple had a teenage daughter who was very nice and respectful. They make it into the Hall of Fame for their graciousness. They had to contend with many potential buyers going into their private space as I was selling one of my final residential rentals. They couldn't have been more pleasant and accommodating (see *Good Chips In the Tenant Cookie Jar section*).

Woman Afflicted with Hoarding Disorder

She was a fiction writer and was recently widowed. She had a small trust fund which helped her get approved to rent by me.

I verified those claims to be facts. Everything that followed I would have liked to have been fiction.

Let's call her Clarissa. When Clarissa moved in she invited all her friends to come see her new apartment loft with 20-foot ceilings and brick walls. It was a very festive affair.

As one of her male friends was leaving, he put his hands on my shoulder, looks me in my eyes and says, "you are a really nice guy!" I was left there wondering why this guy said that to me.

Well, the answer came six months later as things started to clutter in every available walking space in the apartment. At first, it just looked as though she was becoming messy. By the time I evicted her for not paying her rent and regained control of my rental, there would be no space to walk. Furniture was piled high to the ceiling, the kitchen was infested with gnats and flies, and dishes which had been there for a month overflowed in the sink. Food was rotting in the refrigerator and there were bags and packages of new items with receipts which had never been opened.

It took a full 16 hours one Saturday, a hazmat suit and a dumpster which was filled to the brim to clean that place and get it back to habitable condition. A neighbor who saw me in the hazmat suit asked me if someone had died in there.

Wonderful Section 8 Tenant

Madeline was a great mom and a very good tenant. She had three adult sons living on their own and was in school working towards a nursing certificate. It was taking her longer than she wished to complete the program as she had some chronic health issue that would incapacitate her every so often.

She kept the place immaculately, and it was always a joy to deal with her. I wrote a recommendation letter for her to secure a new place to live that was closer to her mother so that she could care for her.

Engineers Attracted to Brick and Wood

In 2013 I purchased a condominium in the American Thermos Bottle Company Laurel Hill Plant in Norwich, CT. It is "historically significant as the primary factory for the Thermos bottles that enabled the company to dominate in the world market. It is also historically significant as an example of the Norwich community coming together to attract the company and diversify the local industry. The plant was the primary factory where Thermos bottles were manufactured from raw materials between 1913 and 1984." The manufacturing plant was renovated and repurposed into loft-style apartments in 1989 as cited on the Wikipedia website.

It was one of my favorite rentals as it displayed the original factory's brick walls and overlooked the Thames River. The developer built beautiful wood stairs, cabinets, a massive walk-in closet with custom cabinets in it and the bathroom.

The brick, wood and manufacturing history seemed to attract local engineers. They loved the place, and it always rented quickly. One of the engineers had to move for a job. When he returned to the area, he contacted me to try to re-rent the unit as he loved it so much. Unfortunately, I was in the middle of a lease agreement term with a different engineer.

Summary

You have now read about my wonderful plethora of Hall of Fame people with whom I have interacted over the last twenty years. Many remain in touch with me and are forever a bright memory in the residential landlord chapter of my life. There are a few who I would like to forget. Notwithstanding that comment, it has been the most difficult experiences that have caused me to grow as an individual, a landlord and real estate investor.

Lease Agreements

The lease agreement is the legally binding document between you and a tenant where the services you provide are detailed, and in exchange for the landlord's services, compensation is paid by the tenant for such services. In addition, you both have other obligations which should be expressly stated in such document.

If your tenant/landlord relationship should result in a court session, the lease obligation will be one of the primary documents the judge will want to read. As such, I recommend that your lease be originally crafted by a legally licensed real estate attorney within your state, and to thereafter, have it occasionally reviewed by such person for law changes.

That public service announcement is being fueled by a recent interaction with a new landlord who was sharing a potential tenant issue and when I asked what the lease agreement stated, he responded that he did not execute one with the person. I gasped and looked frightened as this new landlord had no idea of all the potential fallout could result from not executing a lease with the tenant.

What follows are select provisions which I have found to be extremely helpful:

Multi-Year Leases

The commercial lease standard is written to cover five-to-ten-year timeframes while residential leases are for a one-year or month-to-month period. Shorter leases lead to lots of wear and tear on your rental if tenants are always moving every year or two.

Over the duration of a longer lease period, you will have the opportunity for better profitability. As such, I usually start with a one-year lease term. Then after getting a good sense of the tenant and I have a good tenant/landlord relationship, I will provide incentives for a longer lease tenure.

The most direct way to secure a longer tenure is to extend a rent increase over a few years instead of the rent increase all being applied in one year. For instance, you want to increase the rent by $75 per month to $1,500 per month from $1,425 per month. You could put into the lease that if they sign lease with a two-time period of tenancy that the rent will increase to $1,465 in the first year and to $1,500 in year two.

No Subletting

The lease should have a provision which clearly states that the tenant cannot sublet the lease or allow anyone to live there without prior landlord approval. My leases clearly state who are the current occupants. Anyone not included in that lease provision which entitles them to live in and use the rental, and the person who is planning to stay in the rental longer than a month, must be approved by me prior to such stay.

Two-Tier Late Fee Structure

My leases include a lease agreement provision that states the first late fee is due if you pay the rent after the grace period. An additional late fee becomes due if you still have not paid the rent 11 days after the grace period. This provision serves two purposes. The first one is to provide a disincentive to pay the rent 11 days after the grace period. The second one is to discover who will be chronically late and unable to catch up on being punctual with the monthly rent payment. What I have learned by utilizing this provision is that people who are so late that they have triggered my second late fee will not be able to catch up and are then habitually late paying the rent each month.

No Checks

This is the digital age. Do not accept checks from your tenants! Need I state that any clearer? What additional words do I need to write for you to understand not to accept checks? The next chapter of this book highlights an array of ways to receive your rent payments digitally every month.

Allow for Inspections

You want to visit your rental property at least once per year to see what is broken and needs repairs and to see how your tenants maintain the rental. The lease provision should state that the landlord can visit the rental for inspection within 24-hours of being notified of request for an inspection. That way you are only finding a convenient date but not asking permission to visit.

An additional way to ensure that you see the place twice a year is to schedule a visit 6 months before the lease expiration date. Then when it is time to renew the lease agreement, you can get the new lease agreement signed by them at the rental in your presence. While you are there, you will be able to observe the condition of the rental.

Get Advance Permission to Show the Rental to Prospective Tenants within 24-Hours of Notice

Unfortunately, one day your tenants will inform you that they do not intend to renew the lease and are seeking a new living space. When I first started became a landlord I would wait until the tenants moved out before showing the rental to prospective tenants. Some tenants did not clean the place thoroughly or tell me about broken items in the rental. Then I would spend a week getting the rental back to move-in condition. By adding a provision in the lease whereby they agreed to allow me to show the rental property to new prospective tenants within 24 hours' notice, I discovered that the turnover time between tenants could be drastically shortened and sometimes eliminated.

Showing a rental prior to the current tenants moving out became part one of my two-part process to turn around or get a place into move-in condition within one day. That one-day turnaround kept the net rental income flowing without missing a month between tenants.

Allow for Emergency Entry

Waterpipes break and all kinds of unimagined situations occur. Accordingly, my emergency entrance provision states "the Landlord may enter the property in the case of an emergency without your prior consent."

Summary

The above-listed lease provisions were not intended to be exhaustive but thought-provoking. You should seek a competent local real estate attorney for an updated and legally viable lease agreement.

Electronic Payments

In the Property Management chapter of this book, I established that accepting checks is like using a rotary dial phone instead of a modern push button phone. It is just inefficient. This is the digital age and in the digital age one receives and sends money electronically. It is much more efficient, safer and expedient than dealing with paper checks. Accordingly, you should decide which of the electronic payments methods is best for you.

Tenant Sends It Preauthorized from Their Bank

The tenant would complete the necessary paperwork to have the rent sent to you on a selected date to your bank account. The major downside is that you would have to share your bank account information with many tenants over time.

Your Bank Preauthorizes Payment from Tenant's Bank

The landlord would complete the necessary paperwork to have the rent transferred from the tenant's bank account. The major downside is that some tenants will not want to share their bank account information with you.

Zelle

Zelle allows people to send money to each other using their email address or cell phone number. Both parties need to have eligible bank checking or savings accounts at one of the over 2,300 banking and credit union institutions according to the Zelle website. Everyone's personal account information stays secure as you don't need to provide it to the other person to receive or send money.

PayPal and Venmo

These two payment processors are related companies. They are both easy to use and allow for confidentiality of bank account information as people are identified by their email address or cell phone number.

Rent Payment Portals

Zillow, eRentPayment, PayYourRent, Innago, AppFolio, TurboTenant, Rentec Direct, DoorLoop, and Avail. Those websites offer to assist the landlord in collecting rent electronically. Some are more complete property management systems which also allow you to share your new lease agreement with the tenant or electronic notifications of tenant repair requests needed.

Summary

Getting your rent payments couldn't be easier today than when I first started my rental business. There are so many options to explore. Some have a cost while others do not. You must find one that best fits your rental operation's needs. Just don't solely focus on the costs of the services but also weigh your decision on the total benefits provided by the electronic payment service provider.

Three Burners Not Four

I once had a tenant move in and he shared that the oven was not working. I asked him when I could come over to look at it. After scheduling it, I arrived there and assessed the situation.

What I oddly discovered was that the oven worked perfectly fine. However, a few of the stove top burners weren't working as a result of normal wear and tear. I made a trip to Home Depot to purchase three coiled stove top burners along with three chrome plated grease catchers. I replaced them and the tenant was happy that they could now use the full stove.

Andrea called me after I had completed my work, and I was leaving out of the rental property hallway. She asked me where I was because of the echoing sound of my voice on the phone. I explained the background of what I had just done for my tenant and she said "You only replaced three of the four burners? Aren't you going to replace the fourth one?" I replied that it was still functioning properly and was only five years old. She said "Really!"

I went on to explain that most landlords operate on thin profit margins and there are years when you have more repairs than other years. In fact, this was one of those years with more repairs, as the prior tenant had not told me that I needed to replace several things, and whose costs were now totaling thousands of dollars for the rental property.

I have pride in my properties and replace things when they break or are really worn. The prior tenant's lack of communication regarding the repairs needed deprived me of the chance to not only make the repairs in a timely manner, but also the chance to better plan for them.

I had been managing my properties for decades at that point. In the early days too many repairs in a given year would erase that year's net income or profit. Therefore, I created a maintenance plan that spread out the costs to keep my rental properties profitable. If there is *no profit*, there is *no income*!

Maintenance Plan/Reinvestment

Landlords who spend all the net income and do not create a reinvestment plan to keep their rental properties in good condition and appealing to the current tastes of renters in their local market are being "pennywise and pound foolish" in the long run.

What will inevitably happen over a decade is that they will become out of step with the current home decorating trends like having one of those green avocado refrigerators (they were built better than tanks). My parents bought one when I was a baby and it was still working and useful after forty years. If we consider its low energy efficiency rating, that alone may be a good reason to replace it after twenty years.

How about those 70's green and orange shag rugs? How quickly did they become outdated?

Nice white appliances can be fine unless you are in a rental market area where all your competitor landlords are offering apartments with stainless steel appliances at your same monthly rent. Which would most people prefer? Never forget that you are in a competition to keep your rental property leased and providing you with an acceptable, market-based net rental income.

Create a realistic 10-to-15-year plan to replace refrigerators, dishwashers (you will be very lucky to have a new one last for 5 years), air conditioners, and stoves. I know that I will really age myself by my next statement. At the risk of sounding like your grand uncle, I am going to state it. They Don't Make 'em Like They Use To!

If you still have carpet, get rid of it now! The new vinyl floors can take the wear and tear better and they, are so much easier to keep clean. I used to clean carpets between tenants moving in and out. It would require two to four hours of my time depending upon whether the prior tenants wore shoes inside the rental or not. This is another task which would slow down the turnaround time needed for me to allow a new tenant to move in.

Neutral Colors: Beiges, Grays, Whites

When I first started being a landlord, I would repaint the entire place after a tenant vacated my rental. Wear and tear from a person living normally precipitated the need for painting – little scratches in the wall, holes from hanging pictures and peeling paint.

I learned that it was less costly, more time efficient (remember my *modus operandi* became to turn around a place to be re-rented in one day) and less effort by picking one neutral color for all of rentals. Then, I would only need to paint those wear and tear spots and be done. **Genius move**!!!

Painting is a task which takes lots of time even in a 750 square foot place. In addition, it also allowed me to purchase paint in larger quantities at a lower cost per ounce. I would store the large containers of paint and have them ready for any of my local rentals. Without this change, one day Turnarounds for new tenants could never have happened.

Summary

My hope for this chapter is that it helped you realize the highlights of it were items that sustain your net rental income. While many landlords operate on small margins, it is extremely important to spend the money to make repairs, to replace and upgrade appliances, and paint your rental properties on a planned basis. The longer you defer these items, the higher the ultimate costs.

While my *modus operandi* was to replace things with a "Three Burner" mindset or to only fix what was broken, I did upgrade, replace and improve the appearances of my rental properties over various periods of time. That execution of maintenance and improvements allowed me to remain competitive and to increase rents when my expenses increased or the rental property market dictated higher tents. The planned maintenance and improvements ultimately allowed me to keep my rental properties attractive relative to other competing rental options within my rental property markets.

Property Insurance

Do I believe in having property insurance? Absolutely! Oh, you say yeah, yeah, you are biased as I have grown up in the metropolitan area of the Insurance Capital of the World (Hartford, CT for those not aware), studied insurance as a finance major, and worked for insurance companies. Nevertheless, my life experiences have informed me more than anything that I studied in school or learned from working in the insurance industry. The best way for me to really convey its importance is with a few stories.

My Recurring Scary Story - If It Were Only a Nightmare *

*{This chapter was originally submitted by me for an article in *Common Interest* magazine Volume XIX: Issue 7, 2024 – The Official Publication of CAI-Connecticut. The article has been approved for reprint by CAI-CT.}

Not Once, But.......

On November 5, 2016, I received a call from Alex. He said "Eric, the building where your condominium is located is on fire! I said "what?" "He responded that it is on the news now." I jumped into my car with my heart racing as I completed the usual 15-minute drive from my home to the rental in almost half the time.

I thought that I must be asleep and dreaming, but I was completely awake, and it was daytime. I was sweating profusely as I was hoping that no one was hurt. While on my way there I got a call from Matthew who was also telling me about the fire. He let me know that his nephew and his nephew's wife had gotten out of my unit safely.

Once I got there, I saw lots of people outside on the lawn. Matthew approached me and told me that a lady in the downstairs corner condominium unit was smoking, fell asleep and awoke to fire and smoke in her unit. She ran out of her condominium unit. Unfortunately, she left her oxygen tank inside. The fire ignited the tank, there was a whoof sound, the fire raged up and across the upper level of the condominium building.

I stood there happy that no one was injured, and that the fire department and paramedics only needed to apply an oxygen mask to the lady who was responsible for the fire. It was a sad sight, and it seemed unreal.

I started thinking of the hard work that I recently had resurfacing the wood floor. It was my first time redoing hardwood floors, and it came out looking absolutely, beautiful. Not just to my liking, but to my tenants as well. Reconstructing the building would take approximately two and half years due to changing electrical wiring codes, upgrades required by the utility companies, and the insurance company requiring certain payments to be made only after the condominium association paid for them first.

Unfortunately, this wasn't my first fire experience. My long tenure as a landlord and real estate investor has been singed with three such experiences. On March 10, 2016, a condominium unit in West Hartford in the same building in which I owned a condominium caught fire in the middle of the night. My unit did not suffer any direct damage. As bad luck would have it, the town fire and health departments declared that the asbestos in the building ceilings had been compromised, and as a result the entire building would have to be closed to all inhabitants while the asbestos was removed.

My last fire experience was January 2, 2020, when one of my condominiums in North Carolina would be set ablaze. I received a call from the property manager that "there was a fire in your property." Words I never want to hear again!!!!

The only difference from the other two times would be that this time it would be my tenants who were at fault. They started the fire by failing to inform the property manager that the dryer was making weird noises a few days earlier and by not discontinuing its use.

The fire department came and dowsed the four units in that building to contain the fire. All four units in the building were fire-damaged and severely water-damaged. It would take almost a year and a half to rebuild the structure. The only good news was that no one was injured.

Bad Luck

How could I be so unlucky? I have asked myself that question so many times. Who else has been unlucky enough to have had three of their properties experience the aftermaths of a fire in some capacity within a four-year expanse of time? Oh, how unfortunate your circumstances are if you can match or surpass my regrettable claim!

Accordingly, I decided to ask fellow members of a landlord association to which I belonged at the time how many fires each member had experienced. Interestingly, there were some members who had experienced one fire. However, no one could beat my three occurrences. What makes that fact more interesting is that a few members owned a vastly greater number of rentals than me.

Please Tell Me That It's Not Happening Again

In March of 2025 in the middle of the day, I received a text from a condominium association board member saying that the fire alarm in one of the buildings was going off and that the South Windsor fire department had arrived. I became tense and I instantly could feel my heart beating very fast as the nightmares (or daymares) of yesteryear quickly flashed before me.

Then I received a text message from one of my tenants to call him as soon as I could! It turned out that my tenants had overcooked their dinner and the fire alarm in the building was triggered. I let the other board members know what had transpired and we all were relieved!

Landlord Coverage

All three fires happened in my rental condominiums, not my single family or multi-unit rentals. Why is that relevant? Well with condominiums the way claims work for restoring the edifice is different. The condominium association master insurance policy is the primary coverage, and the individual condominium owner's policy is secondary. In fact, usually the individual condominium owner's insurance will cover the deductible of the master insurance policy. The condominium owner's policy would also cover their personal property, and anything not attached to the building. The best way to understand "anything attached "is to visualize what would happen if you were to flip the condominium upside down.

Typically, landlord insurance policies also cover **loss of rents**. In all three of my fires, I received a claim in the amount of the total rent that I would have received had the fires not occurred. The insurance policies covered up to 12 months of loss rent. I have included a copy of the letters received from one insurance company with the amount of claim checks in the Appendix. The insurance company gave me part of the claim amount and sent the other portion to my mortgage company.

Liability Coverage for a Litigious Society

Liability coverage of at least **$1,000,000** is another important insurance coverage to get. That coverage saved me from a threatened lawsuit from the attorneys for the condominium association of my North Carolina fire. They sent me a letter stating that I was responsible for over $200,000 in damage from the fire on January 2, 2020, and they were seeking it directly from me.

I called my insurance broker and advised him of the situation. He said that he would get in touch with the insurance company for my property. The next day an attorney from North Carolina called and said that she represented my property insurer. Then she wanted me to share the letter with her and all the facts that I knew about the fire. After I finished speaking, she cited some North Carolina statutes and said that she would be in touch with me.

Let me not prolong this story and share with you that I did not go to court, pay court fees, lose my assets, receive another threatening letter from that association's attorney and, in fact, I have never heard anything about the matter ever again!!! Now, the money that I spent on those insurance policy premiums was some of the most important money that I have spent to date😊.

Replacement Coverage

Oh, you think that you are fully covered for damage to your rental property? **Be sure** that you read very carefully or ask your insurance broker to ensure that **you have full replacement coverage**. What do I mean? Well, insurance company policies state they will cover certain things when various perils happen.

However, the next important question is at what costs? Is it actual costs less depreciation or will they rebuild your rental property for the costs then required at the time it is damaged. The difference between those two values can be the difference between getting your rental property back to usable condition and it sitting there, severely damaged, until you can save or borrow its difference.

Summary

I know that there are people who despise making insurance premium payments. They rationalize that they aren't getting anything from making these monthly payments year after year after year.

You should remember that most people do not have the resources to fully self-insure the replacement value of their possessions. Insurance provides what is referred to as a pooling of losses over a larger number of people. This concept executed well by insurance companies and their actuaries allows most of us to recover from when bad things happen to us and our property.

Let my stories in this chapter serve as a reminder that the entire point of purchasing insurance coverage is to have back-up protection in case that guy "Murphy" shows up in your life to practice his "law".

Pathway for Millennials, Gen Z and Gen Alpha

Real Estate Has Gotten Really Expensive

Purchasing **real estate is** not only **expensive** on an absolute basis, but on a relative basis as well. We only need to go back to January 2000 to see that at that time the average annual income was $41,148 according to the U.S. Census report. While the **median home price** was $289,000 in 2020. Now it is approximately **$441,000** according to U.S. News website article titled and dated, respectively, ***2025-2030 Five-Year Housing Market Predictions*** July 9, 2025, at 11:14 AM. The current average income is $83,730 for 2024 according to the U.S. Census Data and Maps website.

Uncle Rick

Please call me Uncle Rick as I am going to give you advice as though I were your "blood" uncle and you will never forget it. Well, at least that is my hope. I am going to share a strategy for Gen Z and Gen Alpha to implement to buy a home for them to live and then for them to become landlords, and ultimately passive real estate investors.

Time for a Dinner Party

Well, nieces and nephews, I want you to organize a dinner party with some of your friends. At that dinner, say "we should **purchase a home** together." I can hear the anticipated "What?" Now, say: "You heard me accurately." "We should pool our money together for us to all buy a home together. That way we can stop renting and begin to build equity."

Pooled Rental Equity ("PRE") for 1st Home Purchase

"We can leverage or use that pooled equity for each of us to purchase an individual home in the future by using it as collateral for a mortgage loan on our future homes. Obviously, that may take 5 to 10 years, depending upon your family and individual resources, employment opportunities and the economy. "

First Rental Property

"Furthermore, we can use that first property to become a rental property as we begin to move out to purchase another property which will become our home. Eventually, none of us will live in the original home and everyone living in it will be our tenants. Then we will be using our **PRE**".

Hire Third-Party Property Management

"We can then decide whether we are comfortable and capable of being good competent and fair landlords or we can hire a professional property manager to oversee its management".

Operate It Like a Business

"We can create an LLC in which we will all be members. Then open a bank account with the LLC as the owner. All rent payments will be paid into that bank account using an electronic payment method and all expenses will be paid from that account. Every month the bank account statement will show us where the money has gone.

As the bank account accumulates a balance consistently each month, we can then open a savings account in the LLC's name to transfer about three months of the rental property's expense into it as a reserve or emergency fund.

Once the reserve fund is established, we now can begin to receive net rental income dividends by splitting it equally amongst us. We can use a landlord portal service to send us each our portion of the net rental income monthly directly to our personal bank accounts."

Summary

The **PRE pathway forward** may be needed for many of the youngest **Millennials, Gen Z'ers and Gen Alphas** for **home and rental property ownership** in the near future. The current price appreciation has reached an apex where real estate ownership is out of their reach without family loans and gifts, which have been taking place more frequently than in the past as many of my mortgage brokers friends have shared with me.

The cool kids that develop a strategy like Uncle Rick has presented are coming to a neighborhood near you soon!

Considerations for Holding, Selling and Renovating

Fayetteville - Everything Looks Nice After Renovations

In July of 2021, I had flown to and arrived in Fayetteville, NC one and half years after my place on Tryon Drive had been severely damaged in a fire, which led to it being totally renovated. I was there to set up an electronic door locking and opening system. The electronic door locking system operated over the internet and the local cable company had alerted me that they delivered the cable equipment for me prior to my arrival and it was ready to be picked up.

I opened the door and liked what I saw in terms of the new cabinets, counters sinks, faucets, toilets and paint schemes which I had picked. I really liked how it looked and felt as I completed my walk through. As I closed the door and was going to walk back to my rental car a new thought came into my mind – The condominium is in impeccable condition, and will I get tenants who will take care of it and value it as such.

I came to the overwhelming conclusion that I couldn't be sure. Accordingly, I was going to sell it. I googled the address and listings of condominiums that were for sale and that had been sold in the last year or so. I focused on the listings for condominiums which had been sold. I noticed a few different real estate agents who had completed most of the sales and decided to make a few calls.

One of the agents, Victoria, returned my call. She said that she could meet me in two hours. I went to get lunch and then met her. I told her that I wanted to sell it and gave her the keys.

I still had a few hours before my flight back to Connecticut and decided to drive by my other rental property on Stewarts Creek Drive. During my drive-by I saw signs of lots of deferred maintenance by the condominium association. Lots of deferred maintenance without a plan to reduce the listed items needing immediate attention is nothing more than a future **special assessment** by the condominium association and based upon what I saw it might easily amount to a few thousand dollars per condominium unit owner.

Special assessments are additional payments that condominium owners need to pay in addition to their regular monthly HOA (homeowner association) fees. I left there and started driving to the airport and ***SELL IT Now*** raced through my mind once again. I called Vicotria again. I told her that I would be mailing her the keys for additional condominium unit in Fayetteville and I want her to sell it also. She asked me where it was located. When I told her where it was, her response was "Oh, I know where it is and I know an investor who likes that area." That investor would become the future buyer of the Stewarts Creek condominium less than two months later.

West Hartford - Things Are Worn Out And Need Re-Investment

I believe that *a portion* of all net rental income needs to be reinvested in the rentals in some way to keep it producing the most income possible for its market. I owned a condominium in a very nice Connecticut suburb which I bought for the attractiveness of its community, the town and the school system. I expected it to be one of my best performers and my highest total return based upon net rental income and property price appreciation. It did not turn out that way primarily due to too many of the other condominium owners not believing in reinvesting into their condominium units or the overall community.

This condominium community was over 70 percent owned by landlords. These landlords were not interested in being involved in the management of the condominium association and were misguided by not understanding that their rents and the values of their properties would be higher if they kept the property maintained better.

A review of the entire condominium community's common elements conditions (referred to as a reserve study) was conducted to identify all the renovations needed and the result was over $3.1 million in replacements and repairs were needed. Many updates, repairs and appropriate maintenance had been deferred for decades.

Deferred maintenance causes the repairs or replacements needed to increase in the property. While you do not see them increasing, they are. Eventually they become noticeable and then you have more things to correct than if you had repaired the original items instead of ignoring them.

Now, the costs of the repairs or replacement will be much higher than they would have been, and particularly, when they become emergency repairs like ones for the elevators. When an elevator service technician is contacted for "an emergency call", his fee is 1.5 times the normal fee. In addition, now the repairs needed have multiplied as their deferral has allowed the repairs or replacements to spread to more things.

One of my contributions to the reserve study project was to painstakingly find three lending institutions which were willing to give the condominium association a loan which would be backed by future HOA fees from unit owners.

The condominium association bylaws stipulated when condominium unit owners can be assessed for special project charges which are labeled special assessments. Therefore, the Board needed to have a meeting to try to get the votes needed to secure the loan and then to start the renovation project. We had a calling campaign prior to mailing the official letter announcing the meeting for "Property Revitalization – Proposed $3.1 million Loan".

The contact information for unit owners was divided among board members to call to educate them on the many repair and maintenance items needing attention and why a bank loan was needed, and how it would be repaid.

We needed the vote by all owners to surpass 51% and that did not happen! The final vote was abysmal. I conferred with the former board president, and he remembered that the final vote tally was approximately 21% of owners voting to approve getting the loan.

I had done what I believed to be the correct solution, and there weren't enough others who believed in it. Within days of the vote, I daydreamed about how the property would accelerate in decline as the elevators had reached their useful functional life probably ten years prior and they were being held together by continuous "band aid" repairs. The band aid repairs would keep it working just a little longer. All the service providers cautioned the board that the full replacement or a partial rebuild of the most essential parts needed to happen within five years.

The community into which I purchased my third rental property was going to quickly become an eyesore in this wonderful town, and I no longer wanted to be associated with it.

My decision was to take my money and run! I had spent time collaborating, investigating and planning how to pay for the decades of deferred maintenance by securing a bank loan. The failure to get the approval votes needed was my signal that it was time to take "my marbles and go home".

It was a really nice condominium unit with beautiful hard wood floors in the living room and bedrooms and central air conditioning throughout the unit. Tile floors were in the kitchen, bathroom and dining room.

Within two months, I made an easy, non-advertised sale to Sam, a New York city investor, who was also on that condominium association board with me. Sam had become a quick and reliable buyer of many condominium units there. My marbles had multiplied since placing them there and I had many years of receiving net rental income. I was happy with this folding of my rental property card at this location.

Atlanta - When You Are No Longer Welcome

I owned three properties in the greater Atlanta area. A house in Lithonia and two condominiums in the same condominium community in Atlanta. I purchased the condominium units on September 18, 2009, and October 29, 2010, respectively.

Everything changes – I received a letter dated November 9, 2018, from the Collier Pointe Community Association Titled "First Courtesy Notice – Request for Compliance" (see Appendix for a copy of it and my response). The letter began "In an effort to maintain the overall appearance of the neighborhood, the Board of Directors has asked us to contact homeowners to remind them about covenant violations so that these issues will be corrected. This letter is being sent to you as a courtesy notice and request for compliance. The second notice will result in a fine. There was a non-compliant item(s) regarding the above referenced property in the most recent drive-through conducted by your association manager."

However, the letter than progressed to cite that I had a "Hardship leasing permit". Such a permit allowed me to lease my property for a one-year term. It also stated that I could apply for additional hardship leasing permits and that I had the right to attend a hearing.

The beginning of the letter must have been a standard paragraph for their normal correspondence, as this had nothing to do with some unsightly thing that the association manager noticed while driving within the condominium association property. As background, walking the property is a standard practice of association property managers exercising their responsibilities properly.

The letter ends with "Thank you for your contribution in keeping Collier Pointe Community Association, Inc., a pleasant and attractive community in which to live." That really got my blood boiling, and I viewed the entire letter as an insult and an attempt to force me to sell my condominium units as I was not a resident-owner.

My reply made the following points of why my Hardship Leasing Permit should be continued until I sold the condominium units:

I want to extend my use of the Hardship Leasing permit.

It is in all unit owners' interest to limit the number of units which are rented.

The condominium association has the right and should implement rules which maintain and improve the quality of life and property values for owners. Such rules should ensure that a high quality of life exists and is maintained.

There needs to be more transparency and clarity around how the decision to extend the Hardship Leasing permit is being made. Without such transparency, the current actions seem like ones solely implemented to produce income for the association by charging landlords a $250 leasing fee.

I intended to own my units and use them as investment properties for decades and now they are trying to force me to sell them. Such forced sales could have a negative impact on the values of all condominium units.

They should consider "grandfathering" in the current landlords, thus allowing them to rent until they sell their units, then requiring that the units only be sold to resident-owners and thereby ending the Hardship Leasing permit.

Real estate owners like me assisted in continuing the long-term viability of Collier Pointe when we were purchasing our units during the Great Recession, and we were the primary buyers at the time. We took units off the For Sale market where there were so many that were dragging down the market prices. In addition, we had to invest capital into the units for refrigerators, stoves, carpeting, repairing ceilings from broken pipes and other things to get them back into usable and livable condition. Those investments in addition to the purchase prices paid for the obtained condominium units assisted the existing unit owners in stabilizing the condominium unit values and starting the recovery process.

I believe in keeping the community very nice and proved that premise by reinvesting in my units which were in stellar condition and very attractive due to my actions.

Due to the threats of not renewing the Hardship Leasing permit for my condominiums and another factor, I ultimately sold them.

Seven Years on the South Windsor Condominium Association Board

I learned a lot about how a board should run, how the right board members can make the condominium community better, how you can be an outstanding steward of the board and community (a nod to Alan) by becoming a board member of the Pleasant Valley condominium board in South Windsor, CT. It can keep you engaged as an encore career (another nod to Alan), and it can be helpful with keeping your rental investment profitable.

How I came to be invited to be on that board is a most interesting tale. It all began when a tenant of the owner below my unit complained to the board that my tenants were making too much noise at all times of the day. As a result, I received a letter stating that I needed to attend a hearing before the board.

I arrived at the meeting with my current tenants, my former tenants and a file that looked like what an attorney would bring to court. After the tenant below made their case against my tenants,

I calmly made my opening statement. I told the board that the tenant below my condominium unit, we will call him Freddy, had lots of history with me and my tenants. In fact, he has made this same claim against almost every tenant that I have had there. He needs complete silence which is unrealistic. Furthermore, I had documentation of how he had handled himself with some of those tenants. Those actions were accounted for in the form of police reports which I slowly passed to the board. I allowed them to get a sense of things as they read threats, slurs and other unfriendly behaviors. After five minutes, they asked that we try to work with Freddy to keep things harmonious for everyone. I agreed to do such.

I left the hearing without a fine and two weeks later I was asked to join the board. They said they liked the way I handled the entire matter. I did not get another complaint from Freddy until I was selling the two rentals I had there almost ten years later. That is a true story, and a great example of how interesting things can happen when you carry yourself in a respectful manner.

Summary

Should you keep, sell or renovate an existing rental property are fundamental considerations for the savvy real estate investor. Does using the IRS 1031 exchange code to sell existing rental properties and transfer the capital gains into a larger rental property, a better located rental property, a rental property in better condition, or a rental property with higher rent potential make sense? **Continuously evaluating whether it makes sense to keep, sell, renovate or purchase more rental properties is part of a good evaluation process** to ensure that your rental properties are providing you with optimal value.

Lawsuits and Time in Courts

Not only have I been unlucky with fires, but I have been unlucky having to go to court four times. Two court appearances were for lawsuits and the other two were for evictions. While I did have more evictions than those two, the others were handled by property managers and the ladies who would become my secret weapon in Atlanta. You will have to continue reading for the enchanting story about them.

Not So Fond Memories in Fulton County Courthouse

My first court appearance was in the Fulton County Courthouse in Atlanta, Georgia (you have already read the ***Purple Walls and Guns on Display in Georgia*** section of my ***Tenant Hall of Fame*** chapter). I flew in from Connecticut and was there for the judge to allow me to evict a tenant. It should have been an easy court appearance with a verdict getting the possession of my property back to me. Well, I did not know that I was dealing with someone who might have done this a few times, and she worked the court system as well as an attorney. Her efforts would cause me to appear in that courthouse three times.

There was one good outcome from my first appearance in that courthouse. When I was leaving to go to my rental car I was approached by this woman. It initially had my mind racing to figure out why she was entering my personal space. She then asked me, “are you a landlord?” I hesitantly replied “yes.” She then asked me, “are you from out of town?”

Now, my sixth sense was going off that this may not be a conversation that I wanted to continue. I started to think she is a prostitute and that she was going to **sexually proposition** me for **payment**. Now, I nervously stated “yes”. She came closer to me. Then she gives me a brochure and says she and her mother run a company that **helps landlords** efficiently navigate the eviction process. She said, “I promise you, you will not have to come to this courthouse again.”

I would use their company, Alpha Evictions, at least three times and she kept her promise. They were an awesome and **very cost-effective solution** for my Atlanta eviction needs. They handled the entire process including bringing a sheriff to serve the papers and to ensure that the tenants were no longer in my rental property.

My Connecticut Court Appearance

I had to go to the Norwich, Connecticut Courthouse to evict a tenant that had stopped paying rent. This was such an easy process compared to the Fulton County process, and it ended quickly with one appearance.

What was not going to be easy would be removing the tons of clothing, food, furniture and garbage that had been left by a tenant afflicted with a hoarding disfunction. My Tenant Hall of Fame chapter details the entire 16-hour day that I spent disinfecting the entire place and getting it back to livable condition. Donning a haz-mat (hazardous material) suit is not my idea of fun.

I Won't Return to Kentucky

I owned a condominium where you could step out of the patio and be on the golf course. It was in a gated community with such amenities as a clubhouse, gym and a lake with a boating dock. I really liked the property and visited there twice.

This place was better suited to be a second home that would have made for a great weekend getaway. As a rental property it started out strong and then fizzled like carbonated soda in a can which had been opened and left sitting for three days.

My return on investment went from good to flat to negative for years. It was near a military base which had staffing drastically reduced and I immediately saw the effects. It was much more difficult to find tenants at the higher rent amounts. Within a year I tried to sell it and it would not sell. I took it off the for sale real estate market and the property manager found new tenants.

It would take years before the rents would increase to a break-even level. Then the for sale real estate market got strong and I took advantage of the opportunity to exit and take my equity home.

I sold it to this older couple from Tennessee who did not have all of the downpayment needed to make the purchase successful. They entered into a loan payment arrangement with me. It was structured to be paid within three years at a reasonable interest rate.

Things were going along fine until one day I received a legal notice to appear in a Kentucky courthouse. They claimed that I sold the property to them knowing that there was mold behind the walls which they removed to completely renovate the property and to sell it. They discovered mold behind the walls only after they removed all the sheetrock in the place.

This was during the Covid Pandemic, and I got lucky as I could appear in court via ZOOM. I received a referral to a prominent law firm to represent me. The judge gave the attorneys a timeline by which to come to an agreement or we would have to begin a trial.

The attorneys would go back and forth for months before we reached an agreement that was much cheaper than the potential trial costs. My only issue with this lawsuit was that people suing me were in touch with me as they were sending me payments for the loan. They knew my cell phone number and could have called to inform me of what they discovered behind the walls. If I were presented with documentation of the mold, pictures and the invoices to remedy the mold behind the walls, we could have reached a fair agreement without anyone hiring lawyers and getting the court system involved. Based upon what I had to pay my legal representatives, I doubt that they recouped more money from the agreement we reached than they would have received directly from me without a lawsuit, as they also had to pay their attorney from the settled amount.

Summary

This experience had a few consequences for me. The first is that I would never sell another property to anyone and provide them with a loan payment arrangement or Note. They spoiled it for anyone else. Someone who loans you money to complete the purchase of your home, probably isn't a bad person. In addition, they would not want to tie themselves to you for the next three years if they knew that there were problems with the property. At a minimum, a courtesy phone conversation to at least see if I would be reasonable about settling the issue would have been a fair approach.

The second consequence is that I will not return to Kentucky as I have bad memories about my experience owning that rental property.

Finally, this episode left something else indelible in my mind which I will leave private.

Return on Current Equity

As a real estate investor, you must keep score using an electronic spreadsheet. I am always surprised to learn that some long tenured landlords do not put all the rental property's financial information on a spreadsheet. How else will you be able to evaluate whether your rental properties are performing satisfactorily and delivering the best possible net rental income and return on investment? I include an example of my electronic spreadsheet in the Appendix.

Total Expenses

For instance, total expenses should include total mortgage payments (principal and interest), PMI, property insurance costs, property taxes, repairs, utilities paid by the landlord, yard maintenance, snow removal, advertising costs, legal costs, HOA fees, property management fees and ***hours expended maintaining rental properties*** (total hours times the hourly wage that you earn in your primary job).

Property Management Expenses

While those of you who are full-time landlords managing your rental properties should use the higher of 5% to 10% of gross rents or your actual salary as the costs of your labor used to manage your rental properties. If you are a full-time landlord, it is the customary fees paid to a property manager if you were to stop self-managing your rentals and delegate those duties. The 5% is for owners with at least 20 units and 10% for owners with less than 20 units.

Account for Time Managing Rentals

I know that there will be landlords who want to ignore accounting for the time that they spend managing their rental properties. I will admit that I rationalized not doing it for years. I finally conceded after a debate with Andrea.

My former rationale was that I was using time after my primary job hours and that those hours after work could not be productively used to grow my income nor advance my career. My reasoning was that I was in a corporate job where I could successfully complete an excellent work product (read as successfully more than meet management's expectations) within a 60-hour workweek.

If you work in a sales position, you know very clearly and can potentially calculate what additional hours working could produce in earned income. Those not working in sales jobs are not exempt from accounting for the hours that are dedicated to managing their rental properties. They must multiply their hourly wage times hours spent on their rental property activities for the year or month. The resulting number is a cost that is netted from rents.

Personal Time is Finite and Most Valuable Resource

Why did I change my thoughts on calculating the costs of managing the rental properties regardless of whether you do it part-time or full-time? Well, I finally went back to the premise of time is one of our most valuable assets for humans. As such, we must account for it being used in our rental property activities. Otherwise, you may be ignoring the opportunity that could potentially be the most productive activity for you, your experiences, and your overall talents. In fact, I could argue that you could use those same hours to acquire new skills and talents. The higher your ambitions, the more this latter point is a valid deliberation.

How to Calculate It

Return on Current Equity = *net rental income/current equity*

Net rental income = *monthly rent minus all expenses (including costs of managing the rental properties by you or third-party)*

Current Equity = *current property value minus current balance of all rental property mortgages*

This calculation is not to be confused or conveniently ignored by using your original equity as the basis of your calculation of the return on investment (see Spreadsheet Snapshot in Appendix).

In addition to your time and return on your rental property investment, you should consider whether this is the best opportunity for your capital. Whether you worked hard to earn it or were lucky enough to inherit, is there another use for that money which might derive at least an equal if not a higher total return than the one you are currently generating? Is there another investment for which the return is almost equal but requires much less effort?

How to Benchmark it

Okay, now that you have a figure. What is it - 5 % or 10%? In and of itself, you might equate whether it is bad or good. However, there are several benchmarks that you should consider using: Apartment REIT returns, bond total returns, equity dividends, equity total returns or some endeavor which when done successfully by you would result in more money than your net rental income. Once again, be sure to include all costs and hours spent (multiply your hourly wage times the hours you spend operating your rental properties and deduct it from rent as an expense).

Summary

You should always revisit whether your original investment idea is still the best opportunity presented to you at that point in time.

A wise person who has a family or who is in a lifetime coupled relationship might also consider whether using some of their rental property time might be better used improving, enhancing or nurturing one of their most important relationships.

To Play, You Have To Be Playing

There are a few unique situations that have arisen which allowed me to acquire properties with attractive investment characteristics all due to me being an active real estate investor. What follows are four stories from my 20-year real estate journey.

How I Found My Second Rental Property

The year prior I purchased my first investment property in a condominium community in South Windsor, CT. I was at my property doing some minor maintenance and I was greeted by a man. He introduced himself and said that he owned the unit across from mine. He started asking me questions and I explained that I was the landlord. He then asked me if I wanted to buy another unit. I said that it depended on the price and terms. We exchanged contact information.

Over the next two weeks we came to an agreement. A month after that I purchased his condominium unit from him. It was off the market and was sold without the involvement of a real estate agent. We still speak from time to time and my nickname for him is "Condominium Al" as he owned about 20 condominium units at that time.

How My Out of Town Journey Launched

If you have read my *Out of Town Landlord* book, you are already aware of the adventures that I had from 2009 to 2012 purchasing rental properties in five states. Well, I explained in the book that the adventure all started because of the mortgage broker I used to purchase my third property in 2008.

One day he called me in 2009 and said, "I want to show you some inexpensive properties in Detroit that you can buy." I allowed him to complete his reasoning and then declined the offer. He waited a few weeks and called me again. However, this time he showed me four-unit buildings in Killeen, Texas. That got my "acquisition juices" flowing and before you knew it, I owned a portfolio of out-of-town rental properties.

You'll have to read *Out of Town Landlord* to see some of the rentals and to learn about the complete adventure.

Unpublicized Offer to Purchase Multi-Family Rental Building

On June 27, 2011, I received a letter in my P.O. Box from a man located in Texas who was offering to sell his 4-unit rental building in Texas. Each unit had three bedrooms, and the building was 4,536 square feet. In the letter which you can read in the Appendix section, he states that he solicited me as he saw in the property records that I already owned two similar rental properties.

Tax Liens and Tax Deeds

On August 22,2025, I received a text message from a real estate agent who I had used for several real estate purchases. Her text message worried me as it contained the words "Legal Notice" (see Tax Lien Legal Notice in Appendix). Only someone who has been involved in a lawsuit will appreciate the thoughts going through my mind and the drop in my stomach as I thought the worst scenarios possible.

I decided to not open the attached file and called Lisa. We exchange greetings and she says, "What do you think?" I answer, "I am not sure as I have not opened the file that you sent to me." She said, "I think there are some properties in there that you might want to investigate further and I will send you the property listings in an email message to make it easier for you."

I instantly regained a few years of my life back from the fear of having to defend myself in a lawsuit. Of course, the irrational thing is that I had not done anything wrong. Nevertheless, I was now conditioned to dread the mere mention of one as my experiences are exemplified in the chapter Lawsuits and Time in Courts.

Back to the story already in progress. I went to the tax lien sale on October 15, 2025. The town had lots of people standing in line waiting to register for the tax lien sales. The town had hired a law firm to manage the entire process. To bid on a tax lien property, you needed to provide a $5,000 bank certified check at the time of registration for each property.

There were approximately 44 people in the town council chambers where the tax lien sale was taking place. What I found particularly interesting as a first timer at a tax lien sale was that at least half of those in attendance were spectators and were there to observe and learn.

The properties which had homes on them had the most interest with many bidders. There was a young couple there who bid very aggressively on a number of properties including one in which I was interested.

I ultimately won two bids for land lots. One was .11-acre land lot while the other is 1.84-acre land lot. There was a six-month owner redemption period. If the owner pays their past due tax liability, penalties plus 1.50% interest for each month within the six months prior to them making such payments, they could retain their property. Otherwise, I would become the owner of those properties. I liked either opportunity.

However, just as everything that I have read about tax liens stated – most of the time the owner who has been grossly delinquent on paying their local property taxes ultimately gets the money together to pay the originally owed taxes, interest, penalties, and administrative fees and retains their property. That is what happened with the smaller land lot. Nevertheless, I earned 3.00% interest for two months.

Barring my relationship with Lisa, the real estate agent who has represented me purchasing several properties, I would not have known about the tax lien sales and not had the opportunity to earn, at a minimum, a nice rate of return on a few hours of effort.

Summary

My active engagement in being a real estate investor has presented me with opportunities which I would never have known existed if it were not for the relationships that I forged during my twenty-year journey as a landlord and real estate investor. By being an existing real estate investor, those opportunities materialized. I most likely would not have obtained them by being on the sidelines waiting to participate.

Ending My Residential Landlord Journey

In July 2025, I sold my final two residential rental properties, and it marked the end of my residential real estate journey. I had gone back and forth on whether I wanted to continue purchasing residential rental properties.

I finally realized that I was no longer interested in accumulating residential rental properties and I had been selling them during the last decade.

I was at the juncture in my life's trail where I wanted new experiences by doing something else with the time which I had been dedicating to operating my residential rentals for almost 20 years.

One of the most fun periods of my residential landlord journey was when I was accumulating rental properties rapidly from 2009 – 2010. During this time there was so much rental property available to purchase in many attractive geographical areas that I thought I should create a Real Estate Investment Trust or REIT.

REIT Dreams

On Thursday, March 31, 2011, I convened a meeting of people who I knew might have the money to invest in the REIT we were going to propose and they trusted me. I rented a conference room in the new Hyatt in Windsor, CT. We had an audience of seven potential investors.

The presentation's table of contents:

- Investment Opportunity
- Ideal Lantern Investor
- Market Opportunity
- Recent Experience
- Initial Portfolio Investments
- Managing Members
- Why Invest with us?

The real estate market opportunity was an ideal climate. There was an extremely large inventory of properties nationwide owned by banks that wanted desperately to sell them fast, as we were in the throes of the Great Recession. The percentage of homeownership had spiraled downward from a high of approximately 70% to 66.9% according to data available as of November 2010. The number of unsold properties was at an all-time high and mortgage interest rates were at all-time lows. You could acquire investment property loans at 4.00% - 4.50% interest rates.

My Real Estate Acquisition Experience Around March 5, 2011

- Property 210 N
  - Purchased at 60.90% of its market value
  - It yielded 26.75% cash on cash within a few months after completing small renovations

- Property 150 Y
  - Purchased at 41.10% of market value
  - It yielded 10.32% cash on cash return on the date of purchase

- Property 631 I
  - Purchased at 76.19% of market value
  - It yielded 63.30% cash on cash return within a few months of securing a tenant

Seeking Ideal Investors Who

- ✓ Pursuing benefits of real estate as an investment, yet does not want to be a landlord
- ✓ Have an investment holding period of at least 5 – 10 years
- ✓ Desires to pool their resources and investment risks
- ✓ Searching for current income in the form of a quarterly dividend
- ✓ Expects long-term capital appreciation

- ✓ Wants to capitalize on the current real estate inventory imbalance
- ✓ Understands investment diversification
- ✓ Is open to participating in geographical real estate investment diversification

I did not get enough of the people who attended my REIT meeting to extend their interest into giving me their hard-earned money, to purchase the hundreds of rental properties needed to justify creating the REIT. At the time, I thought that I should just liquidate my other investment portfolio and go all-in on creating the REIT by myself. It just went against everything that I knew about investment risk management and investment diversification, and I did not do it.

Commercial Real Estate

As I turn away from residential rental properties, my venture into commercial property ownership has shown me that certain aspects of being a commercial landlord are better aligned with my interest in dealing with businesspeople.

In 2021, I purchased my first commercial property and began experiencing having business owners as tenants. Ah, what a difference! The purchase was made to become the landlord of my financial advisory practice and there was an existing meditation business tenant on the second floor.

It was ideal environment as the meditation business met their clients primarily on the weekends and even if they met during the week, they would be quietly meditating! Ha, ha!

There were only two challenges with having them as tenants. The first was that they were part of a national organization who made the monthly payments. While the payments were made on a very timely basis, they caused me to go back decades in terms of the mode of rental payment – they were mailing physical checks. Arrrggh! I had gotten away from that practice long ago.

The second challenge was that I unsuccessfully attempted to entice them into a lease agreement by offering to lower their rent by 10%. However, they would not do it as we just came out of COVID.

Let's fast forward three years and the universe sent me an awesome gift!! I was on a virtual meeting for the local chamber of commerce, and the president was upset as they were informed by their landlord that their lease would not be renewed. My mind raced forward thinking they would be an ideal tenant and business with whom to share space as I was on the Board and really liked the staff. I told her to give me a call later.

After a year of them being tenants, I realized that was a smart decision for tons of reasons. First, I had a lease agreement with a prominent business organization whose presence assists in highlighting my primary business. Equally important, they are awesome tenants!!!

Having said that, please know that the Meditation business owners are some of the nicest people on the planet and I did feel sad at giving them notice to move out. In fact, they would still be there if they had gotten more comfortable entering into a lease agreement with me after being there three years and seeing that I was a fantastic landlord.

Summary

My experience as a commercial landlord has been much less taxing and much more fun. Nevertheless, I am very grateful for the experiences that I have had as a residential landlord. It is in that realm which I learned everything about operating a rental property business. It has provided me with big dreams, so much fun and many friends that I would not have had but for this wonderful 20-year journey.

A Better Endgame

At this juncture of my real estate investment journey, I have a different view on how to progress through the entire landlord lifecycle. Most small landlords or mom-and-pop landlords, as they are more popularly called, start with one or two properties.

Without the mortgage being paid off, the average mom and pop landlord is netting, after all rental expenses, roughly $200 to $400 per month per unit (I know that there those who are not within the bell curve and earning more. Yes, strive to be the positive anomaly). That average can be a good income if one owns ten or more units. Additionally, it could be viewed as targeted to pay for a specific bill like car loan payments or saving for a family vacation.

When real estate is mentioned, people's minds quickly picture all the riches they will have if they own rental properties. However, I believe that is the wrong focus. Yes, owning rental property can produce wealth over a long-term holding period. I define long-term for real estate as a period of 20 years. However, the holding period could be as short as 10 years in an area that is experiencing rapid economic growth, and a corresponding influx of new residents.

Ideally what owners of rental property should strive for is years of optimal and growing net rental income. In addition, I think there should be more thoughts about when to expand your holdings and how to do it in an optimal way.

Die as a Passive Real Estate Investor Not a Landlord

When I sold my last residential rental properties, I used the IRS 1031 exchange rules to transfer them into a Delaware Statutory Trust or DST. The DST sponsor was offering a recently built, approximately 300-unit, apartment building in Charlotte, NC.

I now have a small interest in this new apartment building with lots of modern amenities in a larger metropolitan area with much higher economic and population growth than where my rentals were located.

The best things about this transaction are that I deferred the capital gains from the sale, I am no longer managing residential rentals, I own an interest in this beautiful modern apartment building, someone else manages it, and they send me monthly net rental income payments.

Furthermore, If I die at this moment, my heirs will not be scrambling to take control of my rentals. It is being professionally managed. They will not have to worry about selling those properties as I did it for them. They will receive a step-up basis in the asset value which is free from federal and local capital gains taxes. They will have the option to continue to receive the passive net rental income that I was receiving or redeeming their share of the investment value.

Many IRS 1031 DST sponsors will have a triggering event which will return your investment with a higher or lower potential value. At that time, you will have the opportunity to enter a new IRS 1031 exchange. In addition, there are opportunities with some DST sponsors to exchange into their traditional REIT by using the IRS 721 regulations and performing what is called UPREITing your investment. In this process you are exchanging your shares in the IRS 1031 DST sponsored property into their traditional REIT investment vehicle which holds many commercial real estate investment properties.

Once you have UPREITed operating units, you give up the opportunity to do any further IRS 1031 exchanges. The advantage is that you still have deferred capital gains, but you no longer have to worry about finding a replacement property.

Summary

An IRS 1031 DST exchange can be a better path for you as you age to continue receiving lifetime net rental income without the active engagement of being a landlord and it is an easier way to leave the investment value which you have in your rental properties to your descendants as the selling of your rental has been done in an orderly fashion with optimal value.

Conclusion

I hope that you have enjoyed learning many ideas about how to be an effective landlord or real estate investor. I shared stories from my 20-year journey as a landlord and real estate investor. My Tenant Hall of Fame should have made you laugh, smile and be in a bit of horror. Anyone seriously pursuing a lifetime of being a landlord should know that the path is strewn with lots of joy and a small bit of sorrow. If you can adopt many of the lessons which I shared with you, it will be a road filled with more happiness than grief.

Creating lifetime net rental income requires dedication to constant analysis using many data factors. You need to know what is the best type of rental property for you to own? Where is the ideal location? How do I improve the gross rents and lower expenses?

Once you have a portfolio of rental properties you should constantly consider does it make sense to hold a property or purchase more of the same type of property? Should you invest more of your capital into improving the property or should you sell a property.

Ultimately, you will need to benchmark your return on equity to make many of those decisions. The time that you allocate to your rentals must be considered to properly assess what is not only the best use of your money, but of your time.

While operating as a landlord, there is no such thing as passive income. If you truly want to be a passive real estate investor, you should hire a property manager, invest in real estate stocks or REITS or exchange your rentals into a DST.

Finally, you would be wise to consider whether it is wise for you to hold your many self-managed rental properties as you age. Are your heirs able and prepared to step in if you become ill or die? What will they not know or understand? Will they sell the rentals quickly without the patience to achieve the optimal selling price for those assets? Will they be so grief stricken that your rental properties are ignored, or neglected for months? Exchanging your rental properties by using the IRS 1031 into a DST not only allows you to become a passive real estate investor who simply collects monthly net rental income, but it can better prepare your estate for your ultimate demise. It could be a much easier and efficient means to die and leave your real estate legacy (rental property value) to your heirs in a tax advantage package.

Eric R. Judge is an author, a board member of multiple condominium association boards, and a multi-state real estate strategist, operator, investor and developer.

Appendix

March 31, 2014

West Hartford, CT 06119

I am writing this letter first to tell that you I have enjoyed you as tenants. I know that you are moving on with your lives and are not interested in renewing your lease beyond May 31, 2014. As such, I want to provide you with information on your move-out requirements.

I have found that it works best for the tenant and landlord when they move-out and into their new home in advance of the last day on the lease. In your case that date is Sunday, May 31. This way you leave enough time to adequately clean the unit and not rushing to move out and clean on the same day. Accordingly, you should leave May 31 as the day to do minor clean up and to meet with me in order to give your gate card keys, the keys to the unit and mailbox. In addition, we will walk through the unit together and complete the check-out sheet which we all will sign.

In terms of cleaning the unit, the unit needs to be as clean as when you originally moved into it. This will require that at a minimum the following things are done:

- All floors must be swept and mopped clean.
- The refrigerator should have all food removed and thoroughly cleaned.
- The stove must be cleaned inside and out.
- The walls should be cleaned if there is food or anything other paint on them. The kitchen walls must be free of food and grease from cooking.
- The bathroom should be thoroughly cleaned. Using mold and Mildew cleaners as needed.
- All items need to be removed from the closets and the closet floors should be swept and mopped clean.

The initial security deposit will be returned after you move out and I have had sufficient time to ensure that the unit is thoroughly cleaned and that there has been no damage. The security deposit can be used for me having to clean the unit or for damages to the property that are not normal wear and tear.

Please let me know if you have any questions. I can be reached at

Sincerely,

Eric Judge

Collier Pointe Community Association, Inc

c/o Beacon Management Services LLC
Two Premier Plaza
5607 Glenridge Drive | Suite 490
Atlanta, GA 30342

11/09/2018

Eric R. Judge

First Courtesy Notice - Request for Compliance

Property Address: 2456 Laurel Circle NW   Account #: 2456

Dear Eric R. Judge:

In an effort to maintain the overall appearance of the neighborhood, the Board of Directors has asked us to contact homeowners to remind them about covenant violations so that these issues will be corrected. This letter is being sent to you as a courtesy notice and request for compliance. The second notice will result in a fine.

There was a non-compliant item(s) regarding the above referenced property in the most recent drive-through conducted by your association manager:

Hardship leasing permits shall be valid for a term not to exceed one (1) year. Owners may apply for additional hardship leasing permits. Hardship leasing permits shall be automatically revoked if during the term of the permit, the Owner applies for and receives a leasing permit. If the failure to lease will result in a hardship, the Owner may seek to lease on a hardship basis by applying to the Board of Directors for a hardship leasing permit. The Board of Directors shall have the authority to issue or deny requests for hardship leasing permits in its discretion after considering the following factors: (1) the nature, degree, and likely duration of the hardship, (2) the harm, if any, which will result to the Properties if the permit is approved, (3) the number of hardship leasing permits which have been issued to other Owners, (4) the Owner's ability to cure the hardship, and (5) whether previous hardship leasing permits have been issued to the Owner.

Action Needed to Resolve: Please discontinue the Leasing of your Lot. Your Hardship Permit on File has expired. Failure to comply will result in a $25 fine assessed daily.
The Owner of the above named property has the right to request a hearing before the Board of Directors regarding the alleged violation, or may present in writing their case for review by the Board. If such request is not made within 15 days of this notice, the Owner shall be deemed to have accepted responsibility for said violation.

Thank you in advance for your prompt attention regarding this matter. If you cannot correct the condition immediately, please notify me in writing within 15 days from the date of this letter of your plans to correct the condition. Use the Violation Response Form on the next page to address the violation. **Failure to comply will result in fines.**

Thank you for your contribution in keeping Collier Pointe Community Association, Inc a pleasant and attractive community in which to live.

Sincerely,

At the Direction of the Board,

ZeeAnn Parks
zparks@beaconmanagementservices.com
Beacon Management Services LLC

Agent/Association Manager for Collier Pointe Community Association, Inc

Violation Response Form

Please set forth any and all defenses you claim to the Association's complaint, including any action you have taken to correct the violation. **Please complete this form and email to the manager within 15 days of the date of the notice. Please note that telephone calls are not acceptable responses to violation notices. The legal owner of the property MUST respond in writing.**

Owner(s) Name: Eric R. Judge
Property Address: 2456 Laurel Circle NW
Violation: Please discontinue the Leasing of your Lot. Your Hardship Permit on File has expired. Failure to comply will result in a $25 fine assessed daily.

Comments/Response: ____

Signature: ______________________ Date: ______________

Collier Pointe Community Association, Inc Board of Directors
c/o Beacon Management Services LLC
Two Premier Plaza
5607 Glenridge Drive | Suite 490
Atlanta, GA 30342
zparks@beaconmanagementservices.com

November 27, 2018

Board of Directors
Collier Pointe Community Association, Inc.
c/o Beacon Management Services LLC
Two Premier Plaza 5607 Glenridge Drive, Suite 490
Atlanta, GA 30342

Dear Collier Point Board Members,

Il am writing this email message in order to seek to extend my Hardship Leasing Permit to the Spring of 2019. I was totally surprised to receive the attached letter stating that I was in violation of Hardship Leasing Permit and that i would start to receive a daily $25.00 from Collier Pointe Community Association.

While I understand that it is in the best interest of all owners, including the real estate investors like me, to limit the number of units that are ultimately rented, the letter is ultimately "forcing me to sell my condo unit. This seems to be a continuation of bylaw changes that negatively impact the current landlords/real estate investors from renting their units. The first bylaw change was that the owners had to submit leases to the Condo Association for approval. Next, there was the arbitrary implementation of the $250 leasing fee. Then the bylaw change that began in 2017 and which created the uncertainty of whether a unit that had previously been approved to be rented would continue to be allowed to be rented as it is at the complete discretion of the Condo Association Board to decide whether the Leasing Permits would be granted.

The Condo association has the right and should implement rules which maintain and improve the quality of life and property values for all unit owners. I completely believe in that premise. In fact, I am a landlord /real estate investor that has done that in Collier Pointe. I have constantly reinvested proceeds from my rentals to keep the property in a condition that is very attractive and will increase property values for all owners. Smart real estate investors will always be in favor of and interested in doing things that improve the values of their investments and by ensuring that a high quality of life exists within community which results in being considered attractive by all is one of the concepts which they will support.

My issue is that there needs to be more transparency and clarity around how these decisions are being made. For example, I have never seen the rationale for the implementation of the $250 leasing fee and for what the Condo Association is using those fees. Accordingly, it appears to be more of a "money grab." By money grab, I mean that there is an assumption that people renting the units are making a profit and, as such the Condo Association should participate in it. In terms of clarity, all landlords should be given the criteria by which the Condo Association will be approving and denying use of the condos as rentals under the latest changes. Furthermore, those rules should be disseminated immediately.

I originally purchased my two units with the full intent that they would be real estate investments and I am aware that may not be the case for all of the landlords within Collier Pointe. However, for those of us that did purchase for that reason and at the time when none of the aforementioned bylaw rules were implemented, the new anti-landlord/renter provisions are negatively impacting our ability to fully realize our economic investment. I had originally intended to rent my units for decades and the inability to do that will have a substantial negative financial impact. Did the Condo Association Board fully vet this point? I am sure that the response to the question during the discussion was that the landlords would have to face the facts and sell their units.

Nevertheless, forced sales can have a negative impact on the values of all condo owners. For example, if too many landlords/real estate investors are attempt to sell their units once they are denied, there could be a flood of sales at the same time which will negatively impact all condo unit owners. Furthermore, the Condo Association Board should keep in mind that those landlords could be attempting to sell at the same time many occupant owners are attempting to sell. Communities where too many people are selling at the same time are viewed as an undesirable place to live and one of the repercussions may be substantially reduced property values.

The market conditions at the time that the landlords are being forced to sell, on a de facto basis, will obviously have a tremendous impact on the ultimate values of the condo values. I know that this point is always the case without the consideration of the impact of the bylaw provisions for renting a condo unit in Collier Pointe, however, my reason for bringing it up is that real estate investors like myself will not have the option to decide freely when is the ideal real estate market environment in which one can optimize their investment.

Perhaps, it would be a better strategy to disallow any new sales where it will not be an occupant owner. Then grandfather the existing landlords for being able to rent their units for as long as they see fit. However, if they sell their units it can only be to an owner occupant. This approach would seem fairer and would have less negative impact on real estate investor landlords fully actualizing their economic investments.

The owner occupants and landlords can work together to keep Collier Point a thriving community. It should also be noted that the real estate investors assisted the owner occupants in the long term viability of Collier Pointe. If the real estate investors did not buy all of the units that sat for sell for long periods of time during the recent Great Recession, the condo property values would have taken years to recover and the property values would have been substantially lower than they are currently. In addition, many of us found the condos in run down and abused conditions. Accordingly, we had to make the additional investments to get the properties back in a nice livable condition which matches the wonderful community in which Collier Pointe is. I am not aware of the makeup of the real estate investors in Collier Pointe, however, I would guess that most are hardworking middle class people like me and, as such, the hard earned money that is invested in Collier Pointe is a meaningful part of their savings.

I look forward to your reply and thanks for taking the time to consider my comments.

Sincerely,

Eric R. Judge

Vacate Notice

February 22, 2015

2532 Laurel Circle
Atlanta, Ga 30311

Dear Ms.

This letter is being sent to you to notify you that you must immediately leave my property at 2532 Laurel Circle Atlanta, GA 30311("Premises"). You are occupying these Premises illegally. You and I have no agreement in written or verbal form. Your presence at the Premises was without my knowledge and my approval. I only found out about you and you being in the Premise after my tenant, disclosed it to me that he had allowed you to move in and that he had moved out of the condo without my permission as required by his lease. I subsequently attempted to qualify you as a tenant and you have never supplied anything (identification, salary information, former addresses, etc.) to allow me to make a decision on your qualifications as a tenant. Accordingly, after more than a month of no cooperation by you, you are illegally squatting in the Premises and I demand that you immediately vacate the Premises. In addition, the processes to have a Fulton County Sheriff ensure your departure has begun.

Sincerely,

Eric Judge

ASSURANT Specialty Property®

American Security Insurance Company
PO Box 740252
Atlanta, GA 30339
www.assurant.com

December 3, 2016

000174
ERIC JUDGE
[illegible]

Claim Information

Insured:		Date of Loss:	11-05-2016
Policy Number:	CUO822710600	Reported Date:	11-07-2016
Claim Number:	00102096944	Additional Name:	Eric Judge
Cause of Loss:	Fire	Loan Number:	[illegible]
Property Address:	949 PLEASANT VALLEY RD APT 11-8 SOUTH WINDSOR, CT, 06074-4234		

Dear Eric Judge,

We have completed our review of your claim. The following payment has been issued and mailed separately. A copy of the adjuster's estimate is included for your review.

<u>LPR-Dwelling Condo Unit-Fire</u>

Repair/Replacement Cost:	$5,299.07
Deductible:	$0.00
Recoverable Depreciation:	$0.00
Non-recoverable Depreciation:	$0.00
Previous Payments:	$0.00
Total Payment Amount:	**$5,299.07**
Date Issued:	12/2/2016

Payment Made Payable to:	NATIONSTAR MORTGAGE LLC FOR THE ACCOUNT OF ERIC JUDGE
Payment Mailed to:	NATIONSTAR MORTGAGE, LLC PO BOX 6501 ATTN: LOSS DRAFTS SPRINGFIELD, OH 45501-6501

This payment is being issued to address the remainder of your $6,150.00 policy limit. Please note we issued payment for an outstanding sewer lien in the amount of $850.93 made payable to the Town of South Windsor.

Amount of Policy		**SWORN STATEMENT**	Policy Number
		in	Agency Name
$ 6,150		PROOF OF LOSS	
Issued	Expires		Agency Location
07/11/2016	07/11/2017		

To National Real Estate Insurance Group

By the above indicated policy of insurance you insured Eric Judge against loss by Loss of Rents upon the property according to the terms and conditions of the said policy and all forms, endorsements, transfers and assignments attached thereto.

1. **Time and Origin:** A property loss occurred about the 5th day of November 2016. The cause and origin of said loss were: Fire

2. **Occupancy:** The building described, or containing the property described, was Occupied at the time of the loss as follows, and for no other purpose whatever:

3. **Title and Interest:** When this policy was acquired and at the time of the loss the interest of your insured in the property described therein was Owner, no other person or persons had any interest therein or in cumbrance thereon (State exceptions, if any.)
   N/A

4. **Changes:** Since the said policy was acquired there has been no assignment thereof, or change of ownership, use, occupancy, possession, location or exposure of the property described, or of your insured's interest therein (State exceptions, if any).
   NONE

5. **Total Insurance:** The total amount of insurance upon the property described by this policy was, at the time of the loss, $ 6,150 besides which there was no policy or other contract of insurance, written or oral, valid or invalid.
6. **The Cash Value** of said property at the time of the loss was .... $ N/A
7. **The Whole Loss and Damage was** .... $ 6,150.00
8. **Less Amount Deductible** .... $ N/A
9. **Less Amount Depreciation** .... $ N/A
10. **Less Co Insurance applied** .... $ N/A
11. **The Amount Claimed** under the above numbered policy is .... $ 6,150.00

The said loss did not originate by any act, design or procurement on the part of your insured, or this affiant; nothing has been done by or with the privity or consent of your insured or this affiant, to violate the conditions of the policy, or render it void; no articles are mentioned herein or in annexed schedules but such as were in the building damaged or destroyed, and belonging to, and in possession of the said insured at the time of said loss; no property saved has in any manner been concealed, and no attempt to deceive the said company, as to the extent of said loss, has in any manner been made. Any other information that may be required will be furnished and considered a part of this proof.

The furnishing of this blank or the preparation of proofs by [illegible]

Affinity Loss Management
7509 NW Tiffany Springs Pkwy
Suite 200

VENDOR NO 99999 Eric Judge DATE 01/31/2017 000100082

INVOICE NUMBER	INVOICE DATE	DESCRIPTION	GROSS AMOUNT	DISCOUNTS	PAYMENT AMOUNT
20161107012	01/31/17	JUDGE-1	6,150.00	0.00	6,150.00
		TOTALS	**6,150.00**	**0.00**	**6,150.00**

Judge Rental Properties

	Winston Salem	West Hartford	Fayetteville	Fayetteville	South Windsor	South Windsor	Norwich	Norwich
Monthly	NC	CT	NC	NC	CT	CT	CT	CT
rent	$800.00	$960.00	$550.00	$525.00	$1,195.00	$1,250.00	$800.00	$1,095.00
principal	170.70	145.60	83.06	122.16	164.10	148.17	0.00	0.00
interest	110.23	271.36	118.62	103.92	298.24	347.20	0.00	0.00
taxes	67.55	137.59	39.55	51.12	192.26	205.08	145.12	233.33
insurance	60.00	15.00	20.00	20.00	15.00	15.00	100.00	15.00
HOA	135.00	259.00	177.87	139.00	241.00	231.00	325.74	338.00
mgmt fee	0.00	0.00	55.00	52.50	0.00	0.00	0.00	0.00
repairs	0.00	0.00	0.00	0.00	0.00	0.00	0.00	0.00
cleaning	65.54	0.00	0.00	0.00	0.00	0.00	0.00	0.00
utilities	0.00	0.00	0.00	0.00	45.00	45.00	0.00	0.00
legal fees	0.00	0.00	0.00	0.00	0.00	0.00	0.00	0.00
postage	0.00	0.00	0.00	0.00	0.00	0.00	0.00	0.00
office supplies	0.00	0.00	0.00	0.00	0.00	0.00	0.00	0.00
Cash Flow	$190.98	$131.45	$55.90	$36.29	$239.40	$258.55	$229.14	$508.67
Net Operating Incom	$361.68	$277.05	$138.96	$158.45	$403.50	$406.72	$229.14	$508.67
Debt Service	$170.70	$145.60	$83.06	$122.16	$164.10	$148.17	$0.00	$0.00
Cash Flow	$190.98	$131.45	$55.90	$36.29	$239.40	$258.55	$229.14	$508.67
DSCR	2.12	1.90	1.67	1.30	2.46	2.74	N/A	N/A
ROE	3.67%	*	10.53%	5.27%	15.26%	15.23%	4.45%	6.82%
Mortgage Amount	$ 47,490.17	$ 76,114.48	$ 31,631.33	$ 35,735.45	$ 81,174.46	$ 79,625.66	$ -	$ -
Mortgage Maturity	9/1/2040	5/1/2042	9/1/2039	12/1/2039	4/1/2043	4/1/2043	Not Applicabl	Not Applicable
Interest Rate	4.00%	4.25%	4.50%	4.50%	4.25%	4.875%	Not Applicabl	Not Applicable
Purchase Amount	$61,470	$95,000	$41,560	$45,457	$110,000	$103,000	$32,659	$38,863
Date of Purchase	8/31/2010	5/28/2008	8/25/2009	11/18/2009	9/25/2006	4/27/2007	10/7/2010	8/26/2013
Current values	$ 110,000.00	$ 76,225.00	$ 38,000.00	$ 44,000.00	$ 100,000.00	$ 100,000.00	$ 61,744.00	$ 91,276.65
Equity	$ 62,509.83	$ 110.52	$ 6,368.67	$ 8,264.55	$ 18,825.54	$ 20,374.34	$ 61,744.00	$ 89,453.00
Ownership %	100%	100%	100%	100%	100%	100%	100%	100%

* Not meainingful due to market value anomaly

Dear Fellow 4-plex Owner,

Since you are already in the Killeen 4-plex-rental business, I am offering to you 3310 Barcelona Drive for sale before I list it publicly in the MLS system. It has four three-bedroom units with a total of 4536 sq. ft. Price: $137,900 or $30.40/ sq. ft. Cash, VA, FHA or conventional financing is acceptable.

Please contact me by July 7th if you would like more information. Thanks for your time.

All the best,

Kim

NOTICE OF SALE OF REAL ESTATE FOR TAXES, OCTOBER 15, 2025

Pursuant to Conn. Gen. Stat. 12-157, et seq.

The Tax Collector of the Town of Bloomfield, CT having made lawful demand for payment of taxes due me as Collector of the Town of Bloomfield, and payment having been neglected and refused, I WILL SELL AT PUBLIC AUCTION the following described properties, separately, to satisfy taxes, interest, and charges thereon.

These amounts due are as of July 31, 2025 ONLY. Additional taxes, interest, fees, and other charges authorized by law accruing after the last day of the month immediately preceding this notice are owed in addition to the amount indicated as due and owing in this notice, and a jeopardy acceleration of actual or estimated subsequent installments of the current and/or next grand list year will be added prior to the sale. Minimum bids on remaining properties will be posted after October 1, 2025.

There are 17 properties as of August 1, 2025. Book and page numbers refer to the Town of Bloomfield, Connecticut Land Records.

SALE will take place in the COUNCIL CHAMBERS, BLOOMFIELD TOWN HALL, 800 Bloomfield Ave, Bloomfield, CT 06002, on October 15, 2025 at 10:00 A.M. or after registration of all bidders has been completed.

The property will be sold "as is" in all respects. It is now and will remain subject to all applicable laws, ordinances, rules, and regulations including but not limited to those related to planning, zoning, wetlands, health, building, safety, and the environment. The Town of Bloomfield, Connecticut makes absolutely no guarantees representations, or warranties regarding the degree to which the property is or is not buildable, habitable, landlocked, contaminated, worth the purchase price, or suitable for any purpose, or as to the accuracy of any description, characterization, acreage, ownership, encumbrances, address provided, or that the property or its title are marketable or insurable before or after the sale.